To Pat

A woman who
understands what
education is really about.

Joan Thornton Pearce
2-10-79

THE
VITAL
NETWORK

Recent Titles in Contributions in Librarianship and Information Science
Series Editor: Paul Wasserman

THE
VITAL
NETWORK

A THEORY OF
COMMUNICATION AND SOCIETY

PATRICK WILLIAMS
AND
JOAN THORNTON PEARCE

CONTRIBUTIONS IN LIBRARIANSHIP
AND
INFORMATION SCIENCE, NUMBER 25

GREENWOOD PRESS
WESTPORT, CONNECTICUT • LONDON, ENGLAND

Library of Congress Cataloging in Publication Data

Williams, Patrick, 1930-
    The vital network.

    (Contributions in librarianship and information
science ; no. 25 ISSN 0084-9243)
    Bibliography: p.
    Includes index.
        1. Communication—Social aspects—United States.
    2. Communication and traffic—United States.
    3. Mass media—Social aspects—United States.
    4. Library science as a profession.
    I. Pearce, Joan Thornton, joint author. II. Title.
    III. Series.
HM258.W48   301.14   77-94757
ISBN 0-313-20324-5

Library of Congress Catalog Card Number: 77-94757
ISBN: 0-313-20324-5
ISSN: 0084-9243

First published in 1978

Greenwood Press, Inc.
51 Riverside Avenue, Westport, Connecticut 06880

Printed in the United States of America

10 9 8 7 6 5 4 3 2 1

For
GEORGE HERBERT MEAD
and
LEV SEMENOVICH VYGOTSKY

CONTENTS

PREFACE

The term *communications* is so broadly applied that it verges on meaninglessness. If one is introduced at a social event to a person working in "communications," one does not know whether the new acquaintance is a film director, an engineer, a speech teacher, or a lineman for the telephone company. These occupations and many more—actor, audio-visual specialist, writer, publisher, lecturer, librarian, journalist—are all gathered together under the rubric *communications.*

The activities of communication specialists are so diverse that the link that connects them is obscured, and their social importance is generally unrealized. It is hard to see how teachers, actors, journalists, librarians, publishers, and the rest are related in the vast communication enterprise that is the organizing and driving force of the human social process.

Our purpose is to provide a theory of macrocommunication systems, a theory to account for the functions and importance of the communication systems that are most important to human social life. This is the first step in understanding the communication universe and is a necessity for those professionals whose work directly involves them in the operation of these systems.

Communication professionals need a theoretical model. Technical expertise alone is not sufficient. In addition to expertise, a professional needs a philosophical understanding of his activity and of its importance to human beings and to society. Communication professionals need a theoretical model from which to derive values and priorities. They need a theoretical model to direct their expertise and to provide an intellectually strong and consistent context within which problems and policies can be analyzed and discussed. This book seeks to provide such a context.

Chapters 1 and 2 are devoted to analysis and discussion of the macrocommunication systems that create and sustain human social life, with a special emphasis on American society. Chapter 3 applies this theoretical understanding to the activities of American communication professionals. It is important to note, however, that this book is not a technical book intended exclusively for an audience of experts. It is of interest and is accessible to the general reader as well.

Our deepest intellectual obligation is the one that we acknowledge gratefully in the dedication. Our other benefactors are named in the bibliography; the debts are revealed on every page. Special thanks are due Mark Williams, who read draft after draft with unremitting patience. We also thank our colleagues in the Rosary College community who stand to us as patrons and whose support was generous and indispensable.

THE
VITAL
NETWORK

THE CULTURAL BIOSYSTEM 1

The most extraordinary and mysterious spectacle that nature provides is the activity of living things. We see millions of varieties of life forms picking their way through the world, moving toward one thing and away from another, gathering with their kind, fleeing their enemies, feeding, mating, caring for young, migrating. Some even build intricate structures: webs, hives, nests, dams, cathedrals. And the activity never ceases.

Every part of the spectrum of life participates in the spectacle. An oak sapling reaches for the sunlight that shines through the forest canopy; a bacterium propels itself toward a sugar concentration or away from an acid; a dancing bee mimes a scaled map for a journey to a food source; a bat emits a sonar beam and reads the echo unerringly; a chimpanzee fishes in a termite nest with a straw in front of young who watch and learn; a man studies black marks on a paper surface and learns about events that antedate his birth. We find ants that keep slaves, termites that have gardens, birds that navigate by the earth's magnetic field, plants that capture prey, a profusion of constant, life-sustaining activity reproduced generation after generation and adapted to novelty by a chemical *tour de force* that we are only beginning to understand.

The activity and continuity of life are made possible by communication systems. Action depends on the communication system through which an organism maintains contact with its environment. Continuity depends on the communication system through which an organism maintains contact with preceding and succeeding generations. These communication systems are the most important of all biological systems. Other biological systems—circulatory, digestive, respiratory—are ancillary. They sustain the organism so that it can act and transmit life. But the communication systems are primary;

they are so essential to life that they virtually define it. The action system is a stimulus-response system. Sensors detect certain events or conditions and the organism responds to sensor input; that is, the organism acts. The action taken depends on the biological and experiential constraints that determine the relationship of stimulus to response. A tree responds to sunlight by growing in its direction, a moth by beginning its flight, a diurnal mammal by leaving its nest to hunt. A stimulus is followed by a response, and the relationship of stimulus to response depends on biology alone or on biology and experience.

The continuity system transmits survival resources. It functions in the same way for all types of living organisms except one. All living organisms except man transmit the survival resources that the species has developed in a chemical code known as the genetic code. The genetic code ensures that the physical characteristics upon which life and action depend will be reproduced in each generation.

The continuity system also adapts survival resources for all types of living organisms except man. Mutations and the genetic mixing, which is a consequence of sexual reproduction, create genetic diversity in plants and animals of the same species. These differences in hereditary characteristics enable some members of a population to survive conditions that are lethal to others. When the survivors reproduce, it is their characteristics that are communicated to the young and that ultimately become the characteristics of the entire population. If a hazard like DDT is introduced into the environment of an insect population, those individuals whose genetic coding makes them resistant to DDT will survive. Ultimately the entire population will be resistant. The genetic selection feature of the continuity system adapts the bodies and activity of nonhuman organisms to their surroundings and is responsible for the enormous variety of those life forms.

The genetic endowments of all life forms except man include the biological basis for a complete repertoire of actions. Plants and nonhuman animals begin life with a set of biological controls that determine the operations of their action systems. Individual organisms are capable of the actions characteristic of their species because their action systems are tied to biological features that are transmitted in the genetic code. A wasp and a pigeon are capable of performing their complex acts because the basis for their performance is biological and is coded into their genetic inheritance. Their offspring will be capable of the same activity because they too will receive the code on which the actions depend. Even among the subhuman primates action is tied to biology. Variations in action patterns among the different species are always expressions and concomitants of biological variations.[1]

But human beings are different. The genetic system that transmits the biological basis for action repertoires and that enables other life forms to adapt and transmit survival resources does not perform these functions for human beings. Human beings transmit genetic codes that determine certain basic biological characteristics. But human action, adaptation, and continuity do not depend solely on biology.

In all living organisms except man the action and continuity systems are functionally isolated. The stimulus-response system is not used to adapt and transmit survival resources. The genetic system is not used to carry on day-to-day activities; an animal's activities do not alter the code that it transmits.

In human beings, however, the two systems are logically but not functionally distinct. The same system that enables human beings to adapt and transmit survival resources also enables them to act. In human beings the functions of the action and continuity systems are performed by a single communication system.

Culture is the communication system that enables human beings to act, adapt, and transmit survival resources. It is culture that creates action repertoires; it is culture that adapts action repertoires and other survival resources and passes them on.

The continuity system that nonhuman organisms use—the genetic system—has resulted in the proliferation of species of nonhuman life in response to different conditions. The continuity system that human beings use has resulted in the proliferation of cultures but has enabled man to live almost anywhere on the planet as a single species. The human system is infinitely more flexible than the genetic system and makes man uniquely adaptable. *Acquired characteristics are inheritable through culture which may be thought of as a quasi-*

Lamarckian evolutionary system. The genetic system is incomparably more rigid.

There are three basic components of culture. They are found in every culture and they work in concert to create, adapt, and transmit the modes of action and the survival resources of human beings. The first is language, a uniquely human communication resource that is the wellspring of culture. The second is a story system, a complex of interrelated intellectual constructs that constitutes the basic content of culture. The third is a set of institutions that has special roles in the production, organization, and dissemination of the information that is the most important to the cultural process.

LANGUAGE AND INTELLIGENCE

Language is the foundation of culture. The possession of this unique resource makes it possible for human beings to carry on the kind of social existence peculiar to our species. Human social systems are possible only because human beings possess language.

Two men have made unrivaled contributions to understanding the role of language in human society; an American social philosopher, George Herbert Mead, and a Russian psychologist, Lev Semenovich Vygotsky.[2] Our discussion of human intelligence and human cooperative behavior is based on their work. We deal first with intelligence and then with cooperative behavior. Our concern is to show that language is the *sine qua non* in creating the human qualities that make culture possible.

The notion that human beings possess language because they are intelligent is agreeable to common sense. It seems consistent with the way things happen to conclude that humans are able to learn language because they possess human intelligence. We speak and monkeys do not because we are intelligent and they are not. But it is not that simple. It is true that humans have larger, more complex brains than monkeys; but this is not the crucial factor. Distinctively human intelligence cannot be accounted for by simple reference to the size and complexity of the human brain. *The brain is a factor in human intelligence because it is a factor in language learning, not because the brain is somehow capable of spontaneously producing human intellectual activity.* The common-sense notion that human beings possess language because of intelligence reverses the relationship of dependency that exists in fact. Human beings do not possess language because they are intelligent; human beings possess intelligence because of language. The work of Mead and Vygotsky leaves no doubt that human intelligence is a product of language.

The natural history of language shows that it emerged out of a system of gestures. A gesture is an act on the part of one animal that leads to an adjustive response on the part of another. A gesture of aggression on the part of one animal, for example, leads to a responding gesture of submission on the part of another animal. The two gestures, the one of aggression and the other of submission, enable the two animals to accommodate their behavior to one another. Because the second animal responds to the gesture of aggression with a gesture of submission, the social sequel will be peaceful. If the second animal responds to aggression with an aggressive gesture, the subsequent social act involving the two animals will be conflict. In either case it is the exchanged gestures that determine the subsequent social behavior. Such gestures, of course, are not language. They represent a stimulus-response exchange not essentially different from the types of actions of which the simplest organisms are capable.

Gestures may be vocal as well as physical. The acts of animals that produce responses in others may be vocalizations. Many species of birds, animals, and insects produce sounds of one kind or another to indicate presence, identity, alarm, and aggressive or submissive intent. Language evolved out of a system of vocal gestures. Human children recapitulate the development of language out of a system of vocal gestures. Vygotsky's work amounts to an experimental investigation of this process.

From birth vocal gestures that are not language are an important part of a child's life. Crying is a spontaneous vocal gesture of which even the newborn are capable. It is the vocal gesture that initiates the adjustive responses of family members to the hunger or other distress of the very young child. Later, as the child grows and develops, he learns to make other vocal gestures. He learns to make the sounds that he hears in his surroundings and produces responses to them long before he knows what the sounds mean. Animals, like very young children, are capable of both vocalization and thought. In animals, however, thought and vocalization processes follow separate lines of development. Jane Goodall and others have shown that chimpanzees are quite intelligent and can learn a great deal; chimpanzees are also very vocal. But in the case of chimpanzees, thought and vocalization remain separate. Thought is not vocalized. In the case of human children, however, the lines of thought and speech gradually converge and meet. Vocal gestures give way to speech.

The child's earliest associations of sounds with specific objects and situations seems chaotic. Vygotsky calls this early process "thinking in complexes," a stage that makes up "the entire first chapter of the developmental history of children's words." A child uses the sound *quah* "to designate first a duck swimming in a pond, then any liquid, including the milk in his bottle; when he happens to see a coin with an eagle on it, the coin is also called *quah*, and then any round coinlike object."[3] The convergence of the lines of thought and speech is evident, but the word or sound the child uses refers to a group of objects organized on the basis of accidental perceptions. The child is classifying, but the logic of classification is unorganized and its application is unpredictable. Thinking and vocalizing in complexes is not language. Such thinking and vocalizing is too informal and unstructured, too private and personal. Language begins that way, however; many years pass before complexes are eliminated from childish speech.[4]

The process of transition from thinking in complexes to language is slow. A child begins to use certain words very early in life but is unable for many years to use the words with the same meaning they have for adults. A child can say the word *mother* long before he knows what it means. Initially the child may take the word for a name; later he may use the word to stand for any adult woman; only after several years does the child use the word properly to express only the notion of kinship that the word has for adults.

The process of learning word meanings is an experiential process involving continuous back and forth movement from word to concept and from concept to word. The line of development is determined by the meaning that the word has for adults. Adults may fail to notice the process of development because during its entire course the child vocalizes the word in the same way adults do and the complex of meanings that the child attaches to the word overlaps with the meaning the word has for adults. The child for whom the word *mother* means any adult woman sometimes uses the word as adults use it. Eventually the pattern of correction that improper use elicits will lead the child to revise his pattern of usage until it coincides with the usage of adults. With the word as constant and guide, the child gradually shapes the concept for which it stands. When the process is completed, the child consistently uses the word with the meaning it has for adults. He has mastered a unit of word meaning and is in possession of a maturely formed concept that is thenceforth available for reflection and communication. A unit of word meaning and a concept are one and the same thing.

Words do not refer to a single object but to a group or class of objects. Words represent generalized reflections of reality. "Each word is therefore already a generalization. Generalization is a verbal act of thought which reflects reality in quite another way than sensation and perception reflect it."[5] Classes of objects are not given in perception; they are artificial cultural constructs that must be laboriously acquired. Strictly speaking, the concept *animal* includes all animals but at the same time refers to nothing that can be experienced. An animal has neither six legs, nor four, nor two, nor none. It neither flies, nor swims, nor walks. Given in experience are individual or groups of barn swallows, Shetland ponies, harvester ants, and paramecia. The distance from such experiences to the concept *animal* is great indeed. Children traverse this distance by slow, hard stages. The English philosopher George Berkeley observed over two hundred years ago:

> Abstract ideas are not so obvious or easy to children. . . . If they seem so to grown men it is only because by constant and familiar use they are made so. For when we nicely reflect upon them, we shall find that general ideas are fictions and contrivances of the mind, that carry difficulty with them. For

example, does it not require some pains and skill to form the general idea of a triangle . . . for it must be neither oblique nor rectangle, neither equilateral, equicrural, nor scalenon, but *all and none of these at once?* In effect, it is something imperfect that cannot exist, an idea wherein some parts of several different and *inconsistent* ideas are put together . . . for the *conveniency of communication and enlargement of knowledge.*[6]

In the process of acquiring concepts, children acquire human intelligence. Common sense erroneously indicates that human intelligence is innate, that intelligence is somehow present in young children, undemonstrated and unexpressed until the children learn language. This is not the case. Intelligence is not an innate human capability any more than language is an innate human capability. Language is social; so is intelligence. As Mead says, "the whole nature of intelligence is social to the very core."[7] Society endows each new member with intelligence as he learns the language of the group. As he acquires the group's concepts, his human intelligence emerges.

Distinctively human learning or intellectual development is an experiential process that involves multiplying and interrelating concepts. Learning depends upon the capacity to analyze a field of experience or consciousness into named isolates and classes. Learning a science is a matter of learning the meanings of words for all of the objects and processes that can be distinguished; the names of the parts, of the parts of the parts, and of the processes in which the parts are involved. Words provide man with a "power of analysis of the field of stimulation which enables him to pick out one stimulus rather than another and so to hold on to the response that belongs to that stimulus, picking it out from others, and recombining it with others."[8] We teach cytology by saying to a student "just look at this one thing, the cell; now look at this, the nucleus, now the cytoplasm, now the plasma membrane," etc. Then the processes in which the parts of the cell are involved are indicated and named. The same type of operations can be performed with a field of consciousness. We can think about just one thing, analyze it into constituents, and manipulate and recombine. This analysis of complex phenomena and concepts into constituents with names "is essential to what we call human intelligence, and it is made possible by language."[9]

The operations that are involved in all distinctively human learning are the same as the ones through which a student learns cytology. Attention is directed to some specific object, action, process, to any distinguishable aspect or facet of anything. The object, act, or aspect distinguished is named: a membrane, a quark, a wheat kernel, a patch of line and color, a quantity of money, a tone of voice. The names of classes to which these belong are given: cell component, elementary particle, crop seed, painting, medium of exchange, insult. One learns a tiny unit of biology, physics, agriculture, art, economics, or etiquette. In this way human beings learn the whole range of acts and entities and activities known to their cultures. Intellectual development is learning to distinguish, name, classify, and interrelate that which one's culture distinguishes, names, classifies, and interrelates.[10]

As intellectual development progresses, as one enters the universe of interrelated words, concepts, and experiences shared by the group to which one belongs, one begins to participate in the life of one's culture as an intelligent human being.

Human intelligence is the same in all cultures. It makes no sense to speak of one culture as more intelligent than another just as it makes no sense to speak of one culture as more linguistic than another. The linguistic status of all cultures is essentially perfect;[11] so is the intellectual status. The differences are differences of words, concepts, and experiences. Some cultures possess words, concepts, and experiences that others do not.

Cultural differences are often illustrated in situations when people from different cultures encounter one another. In *The Forest People* Colin Turnbull tells of the first expedition into the world outside the Congo rain forest by a pygmy named Kenge. Turnbull took Kenge to a high elevation from which the surrounding plains were visible for miles. This was Kenge's first experience with distance perspectives. He was a native of the Ituri Forest, a habitat so thickly grown with vegetation that it is impossible to see anything at a great distance. At a distance of several miles from the high ground on which he stood, Kenge saw a herd of water buffalo grazing. He asked Turnbull, "What insects are those?" Kenge had seen buffalo in the forest but had never learned to make allowance for distance when judging size. His experience led him to classify the buffalo as insects on the basis of their apparent size from his vantage point. Kenge and Turnbull got in a vehicle and drove closer to where the herd was grazing in a park.

> Kenge kept his face glued to the window, which nothing would make him lower. I even had to raise mine to keep him happy. I was never able to discover just what he thought was happening—whether he thought that the insects were changing into buffalo, or that they were miniature buffalo growing rapidly as we approached. His only comment was that they were not real buffalo, and he was not going to get out of the car again until we left the park.[12]

Kenge's excursion also provided his first experience of snow, which he saw on the surrounding mountains. He classified the snow as white rock. Turnbull and another companion, Henri, a native of the plains tried to explain.

> Henri said that it was water that turned color when it was high up, but Kenge wanted to know why it didn't run down the mountainside like any other water. When Henri told him it also turned solid at that height, Kenge gave him a long steady look and said, "Bongo yako!" ("you liar!")[13]

Kenge classified the buffalo as insects and the snow as white rock. On the basis of the experiences and concepts with which his culture provided him, there was nothing lacking in the intelligence of his classification. He rightly rejected the classification *water* for the snow because the snow did not act like water. Turnbull and Henri applied the classification *snow* according to their cultural experience, but from an Eskimo's point of view, their use of the class *snow* might seem stupid and indiscriminate. The Eskimo has twenty-five to thirty terms to distinguish different kinds of snow. *Igluksaq* is snow-house-building snow. If an Eskimo were told that there was nothing but *pukak* (a type of snow granulated like sugar), he would know that he couldn't build shelter. *Masak* is soft, wet snow found in spring when it is thawing. *Ganik* is falling snow, *aput* is snow lying on the ground, *piqtuq* is snow being blown through the air during a ground blizzard, *aqilluqqaq* is a firmish snow but not quite firm enough to build a snowhouse with, *mauya* is a soft, deep snow. There are many more words for different kinds of snow.[14]

There is no question of the cultural character of intelligence, for intelligence is a phenomenon of words and concepts and experience, not brain matter. Intelligence comes into being and functions through units of word meaning. Without language, intelligence is inconceivable and impossible.

The same social process that gives rise to intelligence also gives rise to human cooperation. As intelligence emerges, so does the ability to participate in cooperative activity.

The existence of a social species depends on the ability of the species to reproduce in each generation the repertoire of behavioral responses that constitute cooperation. A social species lives by the coordinated activity of its members. Collective life depends upon the capacity of individual organisms to produce the patterns of responses appropriate to their roles in collective life. In societies of social insects the mutual accommodation of responses that maintains social existence is achieved through genetic determination of the physical and chemical structures that regulate behavior. In human societies the same accommodation is achieved through a socialization process that is a concomitant of linguistic and intellectual development.

The linguistic and intellectual development of the child is marked by his grasp of meanings. The child is born into a social process in which meanings already exist. Meanings are dependent upon the actual relationships that a social group has to objects, behaviors, and goals.[15] Corn has the meaning *food* to human beings because they eat corn. The meaning of the word *dog* varies according to the relationships of social groups to the object designated by that word.

Some groups relate to dogs as pets and companions; others relate to dogs as work animals; still others relate to dogs as food. As a child learns the language, he comes to understand the meanings of the objects, behaviors, and goals in the social process in which he is involved. He comes to understand meanings through the linguistic process of "taking the role of the other." To take the role of the other is to stand in the same relationship to an object, behavior, or goal as others do. This is not a mysterious process but a simple and ordinary act: insofar as I relate to dogs as those around me do, I have grasped the meaning of dog.

There are certain elements of the meanings of objects, behaviors, and goals that are value elements. An amulet may be sacred or taboo; a hand gesture may be obscene; the goal of personal wealth may be admirable or selfish. The value element of meaning does not exhaust the meaning of the object; the amulet means more than sacred. But the value element is a critical element in determining the relationship of the social group to the object, behavior, or goal. Values are "the cognitive, the affective, and the directive elements of meaning which give order and direction to the ever flowing stream of human acts and thoughts as these relate to the solution of 'common human' problems."[16] The sharing of values is accomplished through the linguistic process of taking the role of the other. Thus socialization is a concomitant of linguistic and intellectual development.

The socialization process is essentially a process through which the individual learns to accommodate his behavior to the values of the group. Among the things the individual must learn during this process is the meaning and value of his own behavior. As intelligence emerges, it includes in its sweep and grasp the behavior of the individual whose intelligence it is. Elements of behavior are distinguished, named, and classified like the isolable elements in a visual field; in this case the field is behavioral. Language makes it possible to conceptualize behavior, to objectify it and hold it before us even if the actual behavior took place in the past or is to take place in the future. Language makes it possible to inspect, analyze, classify, and evaluate our own behavior, to view it as an object. There is "no other form of behavior than the linguistic in which the individual can be an object to himself."[17]

The individual learns the meaning and value of his own behavior through the linguistic process of taking the role of the other in relation to it. Behavior that produces positive responses in others eventually produces positive responses in the individual; behavior that produces negative responses in others eventually produces negative responses in the individual. This is not reward/punishment training, the method used to train a dog or a seal whereby the animal, having received a reward for performing a trick, will be reinforced in that behavior and will continue to perform on cue. The dog will not organize the praise and approval of the trainer into a positive attitude toward its own behavior; it cannot take the role of the other. The child who has been told that a specific behavior is brave or cowardly may or may not behave bravely in another situation. However, he will come to admire bravery and to despise cowardice. The responses of the other to his own behavior will become his own responses. He will be able to isolate and classify brave action as others in his group do. He will admire such behavior in others and in himself. He will strive to direct his behavior so that it conforms to the value of bravery, a value that he now shares with his social group.

In the early stages of socialization the others whose role the child takes in relation to his own behavior are the people with whom the child interacts directly. This primary group is generally designated as the family and consists of the individuals with whom the child is personally involved. In the later stages of socialization the other whose role the individual takes in relation to his own behavior is a collective and abstract other, "the generalized other."

The generalized other is an organization of the attitudes of the whole community.[18] The generalized other is impersonal; it is the value system of the group, an organization of the values that the group as a whole supports. To take the role of the generalized other toward an object, behavior, or goal is to relate to those in terms of the values of the group.

Cooperation covers a broad spectrum of activities from the day-to-day functioning within institutions like the family to the sacrificing of one's life for the protection of all. The continuance of cooperative behavior patterns depends upon the transference of the group's values to the emerging generation by means of language.

Language, then, creates intelligent human individuals who are able to cooperate in the social process. Through language a society is able to reproduce in each new generation the repertoire of behavioral responses that constitutes cooperation and preserves the identity and existence of the social group.

STORY SYSTEMS

The second of the universally occurring cultural components involved in creating, adapting, and sustaining human modes of life and action is the story system.

A story system is an organization of information constructs that describes, explains, and partly constitutes the world of lived experience. Story systems are not normally investigated in conventional analyses of culture, and they have no conventional name. The elements of which story systems are composed, however, are matters of common awareness. These elements assume many forms and have many names. They are called science, philosophy, myth, legend, history, folklore, tradition, scripture, ideology, etc. All of these information constructs are stories. A particular organization of these stories that constitutes the distinctive content of a culture is the story system of that culture.

The story system of a culture is coextensive with all that is known, with all that a culture recognizes as knowledge or opinion. The origin and nature of the cosmic order, the origin, nature, and destiny of man and society, the past as recorded or remembered are all described in a culture's story system. A culture's story system contains its inventory of reality.

The story system is the most important constituent of any human environment; for it is in and through their story systems that human groups produce "the real world." The real world is the world that is known, the world to which social life and action are accommodated. Everything of which existence or action is predicated is part of the real world.

The story system that constitutes the real world is a highly organized system of meanings through which individual and group experience achieve a public and objective form so that it can be dealt with cooperatively or socially. The meanings are created in and through the process of social activity itself.[19]

The interactions of nonhuman social species with the objects and other life forms that exist in their environments are regulated and adapted by biological processes. Termites and other social insects enter into social life as soon as they are born; care for the next generation and for the mound or hive begins with life. The basis for this activity is part of the chemical inheritance received from the previous generation.

All human modes of life depend on story systems. Social insects and other life forms can carry on their lives in worlds that their own physical and chemical structures render common to their kind. These worlds are inconceivable to us; we cannot imagine what goes on in the central nervous system of wasps during a cooperative act. But human beings do not live in a world rendered common by their physical and chemical structures. The common world of a human group is the real world of the story system.

The interaction of human beings with the objects, processes, and other life forms in their environments is regulated and adapted by the story system. Ancient Egyptian stories of the gods, the Nile, the desert, the king—of agriculture, men, life, and afterlife—created the common world in which the Egyptians lived. These stories were organized into a powerful social force that produced cities and temples, armies and priesthoods, hydraulic works and monuments, the whole apparatus of civilization from writing to taxes. Without these stories of reality, of the real world, Egyptian civilization is inconceivable. The cooperative efforts of a social species depend upon collective action in a world that is shared. The shared world of a human group is the real world of their story system.

In order to understand the nature and function of story systems, it is necessary to distinguish two types of human experience: biophysical experience and biosocial experience. Biophysical experience, like the experience of animals, is not directly related to story systems. It is essentially the same for all men insofar as they possess essentially the same physical attributes. The existence of biophysical experience is evidenced by the existence of common reactions. There is, for example, reason to believe that all men respond in the same way to being deprived of air and water. The universality of certain sexual responses and responses to pain also points to the existence of universal biophysical experience.

It is impossible to be certain about the subjective quality of biophysical experience because it can only be described in terms of story systems. If we read an ancient report by one who says that his skin was burned by "the fires of the sun god," we translate this in terms of our story system and say the man was burned by ultraviolet radiation. We might assume that the experience was subjectively the same, but it is impossible to know if overexposure to the sun feels different if one knows it was caused by the fires of the sun god.

Biophysical experiences then are communicable ony in terms of story systems. The effect of story systems on the subjective quality of biophysical experience is unknowable, but its universality is inferred from the common human physical attributes and the universality of certain human responses.

The other kind of human experience we distinguish is biosocial experience. Biosocial experience is experience in and of the real world, the shared world created by the story system. Biosocial experience is the bond that cements the social group and distinguishes one group from another. The differences in social groups are direct results of differences in biosocial experience. The preeminent biosocial experience, in fact, is the experience of being a member of a social group.

Human beings take their experience for granted. They do not distinguish between biophysical and biosocial experience. The two are implicitly regarded as qualitatively the same. Men regard their own biosocial experience as, in principle, accessible to all men whose senses or minds are unobstructed by error, illusion, or superstition. The common-sense view of reality supposes that the real world is actually there as it is experienced. But this is not the case. Newborn children do not experience the real world. The experience of newborn children is biophysical, not biosocial; it is not unlike the experience of animals. Children learn to experience the real world through the education process. The story system is the core curriculum. To the extent that experience is experience in and of the real world, experience is biosocial and a product of the story system.

Let us attempt to clarify the foregoing with a summary of an imaginary disputation. Imagine the encounter of an ancient Egyptian priest and a contemporary European geophysicist. The purpose for the meeting is to discuss their knowledge and experience of the Nile River. The Egyptian says that the Nile is divine; that it "comes pouring forth from caverns which were fed by Nun . ... the primordial waters out of which life first issued."[20] As such, the Nile is a part of the cosmic economy that includes the gods, the sun, the Pharoah, and Egypt itself. The divine Pharoah makes the Nile overflow so that the Egyptians might live; that is the purpose for his sovereignty. This is the way things are in the real world. The Nile is divine; it overflows at Pharoah's behest; he rules; Egyptians live. The priest's knowledge and experience render him certain that these things are true.

The geophysicist says that the priest's knowledge is false and that the priest has not "really" had experience of the Nile's divinity or the Pharoah's control. It is not possible to experience such things, though the priest, no doubt, believes he has had such experiences. The priest's statements represent prescientific thought. The Nile is not divine; it is a natural phenomenon. Neither the gods nor Pharoah make it overflow. The overflow is a natural phenomenon resulting from rainfall on the Ethiopian highlands. This fact is unknown to the priest, who explains the overflow with myths.

When both finish, a moderator representing the point of view of our discussion of story systems says that the positions of the two men are essentially the same. The statements of both men indicate similar biophysical experiences. That is, the Nile is there for both just as it is there for the animals that drink from it. The Nile overflows for both just as it overflows for the animals that run from its flood. But both men have had radically different biosocial experiences of the Nile in their respective real worlds. Each man describes and explains the Nile as it is experienced in his real world and in a manner consistent with the other experiences each has had in his real world.

The attitude of each speaker, the moderator continues, indicates that he has had a crucial biosocial experience: the experience of knowing with certainty. Each is sure of the truth or validity of his statements. Each knows that his understanding is correct because his statements meet the tests of truth. There are only two such tests. The first is the test of corroboration: are the statements supported by the experience of others? The second test is the test of consistency: are the statements consistent with the other statements that constitute the most certain knowledge possessed by the culture of the speaker? The statements of both men meet both tests. The priest's statements are corroborated by other Egyptians; the scientist's statements are corroborated by other scientists. The priest's statements are consistent with Egyptian knowledge, with ancient revelations concerning the nature of reality. The scientist's statements are consistent with scientific knowledge; they are based on scientific method and make prediction or control possible, at least in principle. Since the statements of both men meet both tests, both are true. And the truth of their positions has provided both men with the biosocial experience of knowing with certainty, an experience that is available to all men through their story systems.

The geophysicist has erred in one particular, the moderator continues. It is not acceptable to say that the priest has not had the experience he reports when many other Egyptians report the same experience. To deny the possibility of such experience is to confuse biophysical and biosocial experience. It is to say that one's own biosocial experience is the test for all experience; that one's own biosocial experience is what all men would report were they not ignorant, deluded, or liars. Such a position is not respectable by any intellectual standard.

Let us say that the disputation includes the remarks of three respondents to the moderator's assessment. The first, another scientist, says that he agrees with the geophysicist, that the scientific tradition has proven that its statements are the true ones because science has enabled man to predict and control nature as no other tradition has. Furthermore, he says, if the Egyptian is believed for a moment, nothing makes any sense.

The moderator rejects these comments. They merely indicate that the second scientist defines and experiences knowledge the same way his colleague does. Both have the experience of knowledge or proof when descriptions and explanations are produced by scientific method and enable prediction and control. The moderator also says that, of course, the Egyptian story makes nonsense out of the real world known to the scientists. All story systems are essentially closed systems that render all others nonsensical. *Nonsense* means unintelligible or inconsistent with experience. But what is intelligible and what is experienced depend themselves on story systems.

The second respondent, a Medieval Christian bishop, says that he knows both the Egyptian and the geophysicist to be in error. All so-called natural phenomena are manifestations of and are controlled by the will of the one true god. Nevertheless, the procedure of the Egyptian for arriving at the truth is, in principle, superior. Trusting in divine revelation is a better method than trusting in mere human knowledge, which inevitably overreaches itself and goes astray. The bishop justifies this statement at length on the basis of his knowledge and experience.

The third respondent, a Zen master, says that both the Egyptian and the geophysicist are wrong. The Zen master says that he has no idea what the Nile is or why it overflows, but neither do the others. Their descriptions and explanations attempt to capture a universal world process that is not to be grasped in concepts and language. Such forlorn attempts lead to misery and illusion and to violence against sentient beings and nature.

The moderator concludes the meeting. Both stories have positive results; both story systems have been supportive of human life. Quantitatively, the Egyptian story appears to have the edge. Its life-supporting capability is measurable in terms of tens of centuries. The scientific story has yet to prove itself; it is barely three hundred years old. As far as the quality of life is concerned, both leave much to be desired. But he admits finally both quantitative and qualitative tests are inconclusive depending, as they do, on story systems themselves.[21]

The imaginary disputation thus concluded clarifies the relationship between story systems, human experience, and human environments. It reveals the central role of the story system in creating both human experience and human environments. Human beings do not adapt their lives and bodies to environments over a number of generations like other animals. They create within their environments real worlds adapted to themselves, alterable and communicable worlds that are transmitted not in a chemical code but in a linguistic code. The story system of a group is its preeminent cultural artifact, the mainstay and conduit of its life.

INSTITUTIONS

The stories that sustain life in a society must be produced, organized, adapted, and disseminated. The structures that perform these functions are the major social institutions that occur universally, the religious and political institutions found in all societies. These institutions constitute the third major factor in our analysis of culture.

In every culture each of the institutions carries out its role in relation to its own special type of stories. Institutional structure and function are determined by the stories that are the institution's special concern. These stories are logically prior to the institution. An understanding of institutional form and function depends upon an understanding of the stories that are the special province of each institution.

The most important stories of any story system are the religious ones. They answer ultimate questions concerning the origin and organization of the universe, the nature of the material world, the nature of man, and the purpose for human existence. Religious stories provide the basis for ethical systems, enable social and individual life to be directed to the attainment of ultimate objectives, and provide the basis for dealing with the forces that are inherent in nature.

The primary function of religious stories, however, is to provide a basis for social organization.[22] Social organization is always established in accordance with the cosmic and natural orders. Social organization implies knowledge of an order of existence over which man has no control and to which he must accommodate his individual and collective lives. Religious stories constitute such knowledge and without it social forms cannot be created.

The religious institution in any society is the social unit or complex that produces, organizes, adapts, and disseminates religious stories, that is, stories about ultimate realities. All societies are based upon stories of the cosmic and natural orders. These stories may reside in revelation, in scientific or philosophical treatises, in collections of myth and legend, in epic poetry, or in statements of self-evident principles. Regardless of how they are formulated or packaged, stories of the origin and organization of the universe, the nature of the material world, the nature of man, and the purpose of human existence are religious stories. The social structures or complexes that produce, organize, adapt, and disseminate these stories are religious institutions.[23]

Religious institutions are always the dominant institutions of societies. Though they may possess few or none of the ordinary external signs of power, religious institutions control the organization and expenditure of social energy. The stories they provide direct, constrain, and legitimize the activities of other institutions, which ultimately have no choice but to accommodate their actions to reality.

All societies have religious institutions. The common-sense view of religious institutions associates them with beliefs in divine beings, a supernatural order, clergymen, and certain conventional formulae and liturgical practices. Such a view makes it appear that some societies have religious institutions and some do not and consequently obscures the nature and function of religious institutions.

In some societies the religious institution is easy to identify and the relationship of the stories it controls to social forms is quite apparent. Ancient Egyptian society, Mayan, Incan, Byzantine, Medieval European, and traditional Moslem societies fall into this category. In contemporary Western societies, however, the identity of religious institutions is obscured and the relationship of religious stories to social organization is generally unperceived and unacknowledged.

The religious institutions of the modern Western world are not ecclesiastical communities based on revelations and scriptures but intellectual communities based on philosophical and scientific traditions. In the United States, the Soviet Union, Western Europe, and elsewhere, the stories about reality that determine the social order are controlled by institutions that are secular in nature. These institutions are diffused throughout the societies, imbedded in their social structures—in schools and universities, scientific and professional organizations, and in the structures of governments and political parties. The roles performed by these institutions are based on an intellectual consensus that is equivalent to a secular orthodoxy. Their power is as real and effective as the power of the Medieval Church was long ago.

Over the past three hundred years the intellectual-scientific community has gradually undermined the authority and credibility of ecclesiastical communities. It has taken over the primary function of providing the stories of reality from which the social order is derived. The stories that the intellectual-scientific community produced overturned the old order in the West in the eighteenth and nineteenth centuries. In the present century these stories have provided and are providing the basis for social reconstruction in the rest of the world. Social and intellectual turmoil and protracted bitter warfare have accompanied the assumption of dominance by the intellectual-scientific religious institution. At the root of these conflicts are competing stories of reality. As the intellectual-scientific religious stories are accepted in a society, the old order passes and the new religion reconstitutes the society.

In the West the centuries-old competition between the ecclesiastical communities and the intellectual-scientific community is all but over. The key ideological conflicts associated with the names Galileo, Darwin, and Freud resulted in defeats for the churches. With each victory the intellectual-scientific community gradually assumed control over stories dealing with essential aspects of the nature of things: first the physical world (Galileo), then life (Darwin), then human behavior (Freud). Today the ability of ecclesiastical communities to exercise control over such stories is gone and with it the power to determine social forms. The result is that contemporary Western societies are almost totally secularized.

The religious institution of Western societies is the intellectual-scientific religious institution. It produces, organizes, adapts, and disseminates the stories of the cosmic and natural orders that sustain the social order.

One of the key stories that the religious institution provides is the story of the origin of life and man. A controversy[24] occurring in the United States in connection with this story serves to illustrate the manner in which the intellectual-scientific religious institution pervades a society and exercises its dominance through the social structures with which it is affiliated.

In 1959, the centennial of Darwin's *The Origin of Species*, Hermann J. Muller, a geneticist, commenting on the general neglect of evolutionary theory in public-school science courses, stated that the teaching of biology in American public schools was dominated by "antiquated religious traditions." In order to help correct this situation, the National Science Foundation, a publicly supported scientific organization, set up the Biological Sciences Curriculum Study and provided $7 million to create "modern" biology courses. Three textbooks were developed, all based on evolutionary approaches. The new books were introduced in 1964, and a controversy erupted due to the objections of Christians. In 1972, the religion editor of the Washington *Star*, sued the National Science Foundation on behalf of forty million evangelical Christians, "for using public funds to support education that violated religious beliefs." The perceptions of the objecting Christians were essentially correct. The questions at issue were religious questions. The textbooks violate the religious beliefs of Christians and in doing so manifest their own identity as books dealing with religious questions.

The point here is to note how the intellectual-scientific community exercised its dominance in this case. We have, first of all, a noted intellectual, Muller, giving voice to a conviction about the unsatisfactory character of public-school instruction relative to the origin of life and man. Because he expressed the consensus of his community, the National Science Foundation, a unit of the intellectual-scientific religious institution within the central government, appropriated funds. Other members of the intellectual-scientific religious institution affiliated with universities produced the textbooks. The textbooks were then accepted by still other members of the intellectual-scientific religious institution, the public school teachers, and administrators. The books were accepted because they were regarded as the most authoritative. In the schools the books encountered resistance. The parents of some of the children objected to the books because they conflicted with Christian teaching on the origin and life of man.

The Christians who objected to the textbooks tried hard to do something to protect children from religious teachings that they considered erroneous and harmful. They achieved very little. In

California, critics of the biology texts were able to persuade the state Board of Education to accept some changes. Twenty-one of these changes are displayed in the *Scientific American* article. Their significance is minimal; they are clearly designed simply to keep the evolutionists from overstating their case. Not one could be construed as supportive of the special creation doctrine on the origin of life and man that the Christian critics advocate. Attempts on the part of Christians to get "equal time" for the teaching of the special creation doctrine failed in California and elsewhere. A 1973 Tennessee law requiring equal time for the special creation concept was declared unconstitutional and repealed in 1975.[25]

Dorothy Nelkin, the author of the article in *Scientific American,* expresses the perplexity and concern of the scientific community over the resistance to the teaching of evolution. She does not see that this resistance is based on valid objections to the religious doctrines presented in evolutionary teaching. The theory of evolution deals with ultimate questions on the origin of life and man. The Christians see quite clearly that such questions are religious in nature. Their anger and frustration are manifested because their children are being taught religious concepts hostile to their own religion and they are powerless to prevent it. As one Christian spokesman put it, "under the banner of science, value systems are being marched into the classroom. . . . The truth dawning on parents . . . is that education is a sectarian occupation."[26] Nelkin is concerned that popular resistance to science may disrupt the teaching of science in school. She fears that popular resistance made effective through democratic values and processes may enter into public policy where science and science education are concerned. In relation to biology at least, such fears are hardly realistic.

A better perspective on the textbook controversy and the larger issue of Christian resistance to evolution is achieved by comparing these with an earlier historic controversy between the Christian and scientific communities. Unlike the present case, this other controversy occurred when the Christian religious institution was dominant. The offending story in this earlier dispute was the doctrine of the earth's motion on its axis and around the sun. The offending scientist was Copernicus, whom Luther called "an upstart astrologer who strove to show that the earth revolves. . . . This fool wishes to reverse the entire science of astronomy; but sacred Scripture tells us that Joshua commanded the sun to stand still and not the earth."[27] The leaders of the ecclesiastical communities clearly saw the issues at hand.

Copernicanism was potentially destructive for an entire fabric of thought. . . . More than a picture of the universe and a few lines of Scripture were at stake. The drama of Christian life and the morality that had been made dependent on it would not readily adapt to a universe in which the earth was just one of a number of planets.[28]

Some seventy years after the death of Copernicus in 1543, John Donne summed up the impact of the astronomer's theories.

[The] new philosophy calls all in doubt. . . . Tis all in pieces, all coherence gone.[29]

The resistance of the ecclesiastical communities was vigorous. The Lutheran theologian Melanchthon urged that strong measures be taken to restrain the "impiety" of the Copernicans. After 1610, Copernicus's doctrine was formally condemned as heretical. In 1616 Copernicus's work and all others that affirmed the earth's motion were placed on the *Index*, the list of books condemned by the Catholic Church. In 1633 Copernicus's most famous advocate, Galileo, was forced to disavow Copernicanism. "Not until 1822 did the [Catholic] Church permit the printing of books that treated the earth's motion as physically real, and by then all but the most rigidly orthodox Protestant sects had long been persuaded."[30]

As late as 1873 the ex-president of an American Lutheran teachers' seminary published a work condemning Copernicus, Newton, and a distinguished series of subsequent astronomers for their divergence from scriptural cosmology. Even today the newspapers occasionally report the dicta of a dotard who insists upon the uniqueness and stability of the earth.[31]

If the year 1873 marks the end of resistance to Copernicanism, the controversy lasted 330 years. By comparison the progress of Darwin's theory has been rapid indeed.

The issue in the Copernican and Darwinian controversies is the same: authority to answer the ultimate questions. The textbook controversy is useful because it reveals how the authority once possessed by ecclesiastical communities has passed and is now exercised by the intellectual-scientific religious institution.

The dominance of the intellectual-scientific religious institution is secure. In American public schools the religious stories produced by that institution are central to the curriculum. Physics, biology, and the social sciences are the carriers of these religious stories and are taught in all schools. At the same time, the stories of the ecclesiastical communities are strictly forbidden in public schools. Christian groups recognize the impact of scientific instruction, but they are virtually helpless. Athough objections continue, the Christians are impotent. No unit of the central government like the National Science Foundation supplies millions of dollars to support Christian textbooks. The universities whose faculties produce books and train teachers are committed to science. Finally, the Christian groups cannot consistently support their own cause. They do not urge the abandonment of science. They wish to accept Copernicus, Galileo, and Newton and to reject Darwin, but in the long run this is not possible. Nor is it possible for Christians to overcome a religious rival when the legal system that Christians accept imposes a definition of religion that allows the rival to teach his answers to ultimate questions but demands silence from the Christians.

The Copernican and Darwinian controversies and their sequels have established the authority of the intellectual-scientific community in the Western world. Where questions regarding the nature of the physical universe and the origin of life are concerned, the intellectual-scientific community has no serious competitor.

Stories that answer ultimate questions concerning the material world do not, by themselves, provide a sufficient basis for social organization. Social organization also depends upon stories of human nature and the human condition. Such stories answer ultimate questions concerning basic human characteristics, man's ultimate destiny, and the cosmic forces that have determined this destiny. If social organization and action are to be possible, men must know what sort of beings they are; they must know the purpose for their individual and collective lives; they must know what forces or powers have determined these purposes. It is the function of the religious institution to supply this knowledge.

In present-day Western societies the story of man that is the basis for social organization and action is the story produced by the intellectual-scientific religious institution. The intellectual-scientific story originated within the Christian story. Its development apart from the Christian story begins with the Renaissance; its identity as a separate tradition becomes clear with the Enlightenment. Late in the eighteenth century the intellectual-scientific story of man first achieved official status in some Western societies. The Enlightenment version has been augmented by the development of Marxism and the social sciences, particularly economics and psychology. Although no version exists that is universally accepted in all of its details, there is a general consensus in the West and in socialist societies around the world on the competence of the intellectual-scientific community to hold custody of the story of man.

The other major social institution, the political institution, is primarily concerned with the social order rather than the cosmic order.

Social behavior is behavior organized into patterns of mutual accommodation that sustain life. Social behavior is a common feature of animal life. "It is now appreciated that the life of all higher animals is basically social, that social behavior in its most different aspects is an essential feature of that life."[32]

In all social animals except man, social behavior is organized by biological systems. Nonhuman social life "is governed by anatomy and physiology. . . . Variations are direct expressions and concomitants of biological variations."[33] The social life of the hive is based on the biological systems that produce the physical differences of queen, worker, and drone. It is also based on the biological systems that produce the different responses to scents, sounds, body markings, movements, and gestures, to environmental objects such as flowers, other insects, and the comb. The orderly activities of the hive that secure the food supply and the continuance of life are all determined by biological systems.

In human societies, however, social behavior is determined not by biological systems but by culture. The political institution is the component of culture that plays the key role in determining social behavior. The function of the political institution is to create the basic patterns of cooperative behavior that constitute social organization.

The political institution performs its function through the production, organization, adaptation, and dissemination of political stories. Political stories are stories that determine basic patterns of cooperative activity. Political stories define the group and specify who may participate fully in group activities: the native-born, the naturalized, males, females, persons over sixteen or twenty-one years of age, whites, blacks, etc. Political stories create the categories that express the relationship of the individual to the group: citizen, subject, commoner, noble, comrade, slave. Political stories organize the work that sustains and protects life. They create the moral and legal obligations of workers, hunters, soldiers, merchants, farmers, manufacturers, physicians, and teachers. Political stories organize the distribution of wealth and resources. They determine what can be owned; who can own, who shares, how goods are shared, who is responsible for the helpless and indigent, and who cares for the ill and incapacitated. Political stories determine who shall make the decisions affecting group welfare and activities, how the decisions shall be made, and who shall be consulted. Shall the group expand, migrate, colonize, industrialize, or go to war? It is the political institution that creates and disseminates these stories.

The political institution of a society is not the government. Government is the creation of the political institution. The political institution determines what the nature of government shall be and holds the government accountable for its actions. The government is a part of the political institution. And like other parts, the government generates and disseminates political stories. But the political institution is broader than the government, and political stories can originate in any sector of the society. Political instability in a society occurs when the government and the political institution are not working well together, when the political institution or the government is demanding forms of cooperation that the other opposes.

The political institution is essentially an open institution. Its openness most clearly reveals the nature of the political institution as a story-telling entity. Any individual or group that generates and disseminates stories that affect patterns of cooperation can act as a part of the political institution. There are no formal qualifications. Neither status, wealth, position, nor other qualifications limit membership. Ordinarily, the individuals and groups whose stories have most impact on the cooperative patterns of a society are those possessed of authority, position, wealth, or other attributes and resources that confer influence and power: kings, chiefs, aristocrats, holders of high office, political parties, labor, commercial, military, industrial, and professional organizations. But any individual or group may function as a member of the political institution. Men like Gandhi and Martin Luther King possessed neither formal authority nor material resources. Their power and their influence over cooperative patterns stemmed entirely from the power of the stories they told. In fifteenth-century France, Joan of Arc, a seventeen-year-old shepherd, told a story of heavenly voices that led to a great military effort and altered her nation's history. Her career clearly shows that all one needs to affect patterns of cooperative activity is a story and the ability to tell it.

Although the political institution may employ force, either through the government or some other way such as rebellion, guerrilla warfare, or terrorism, the political institution does not depend on force to determine basic patterns of cooperative action. Ultimately, human patterns of cooperation can only be maintained by stories. Patterns maintained by force not justified and legitimized by stories ultimately fail. The government of South Vietnam in the later years of the war was a government dependent on force. The impact of its stories on basic patterns of cooperation was minimal; its failure was inevitable.

Societies need force for only two purposes: to provide for conflicts with other societies and to make up for the deficiencies of the society's political institution. If the quality of cooperative action within a society depends upon force to any degree, it is because the political institution is failing to provide sufficiently effective stories.

The most important stories that the political institution provides are derived from religious stories. The key political stories are based on stories of the nature of things, which are supplied by the religious institution. Political stories are constrained by "reality." They organize and regulate social life in accordance with the nature of things. It is the nature of things, not the political institution, that determines the ultimate objectives of social life.

The American political institution, for example, did not create the ultimate objectives of American social life. These objectives are not even regarded as American; they are regarded as objectives of human social life in general. For Americans, the ultimate objectives of social life are set forth in the religious story in the Declaration of Independence. The Declaration is clearly a religious document. It provides stories of the cosmic and human orders and the ultimate purposes for social organization. "We hold these truths to be self-evident. . . . All men are created equal . . . they are endowed by their Creator with certain unalienable rights . . . among these are life, liberty, and the pursuit of happiness." The connection between these facts of existence and social organization is made fully explicit. "To secure these rights, governments are instituted among men, deriving their just powers from the consent of the governed. . . . Whenever any form of government becomes destructive of these ends, it is the right of the people to alter or abolish it, and to institute new government." The Declaration asserts that equality, human rights, consent, and popular sovereignty are inherent in the nature of things. They are determined by the creator. By creating a social order in accordance with these facts of existence, men do no more than accommodate themselves to reality, to "the laws of nature and of nature's God."[34] In the twentieth century, belief in the creator has been fully dissociated from the self-evident truths of the Declaration. These truths now stand on their own regardless of what one believes about a creator.

The key political story that organizes and regulates American life in accordance with the Declaration is the United States Constitution. The Articles of the Constitution and its amendments have no other purpose than ensuring that social life is carried on in accordance with the principles of the Declaration. The seven articles create a structure of government designed to ensure that equality, liberty, consent, and popular sovereignty are not violated by the most likely offender, the government. *Tyranny* was the word used by the authors of the Constitution to stand for the transgressions of government against the principles of the Declaration. The complex structure of countervailing powers created in the seven articles was intended to make tyranny impossible. The first ten amendments to the Constitution, which are known as the Bill of Rights, explicate the meaning of liberty, provide for its protection, and seek to ensure that government will not be immune from public scrutiny and criticism. Of the other amendments, six extend or secure the right to vote; one prohibits slavery; and one provides for due process and equal protection of the laws. There can be no question of the function of the Constitution as a political story or of its relationship to the Declaration of Independence. For almost two hundred years the Constitution has applied the religious principles of the Declaration to historic developments within a social system that has undergone tremendous changes.

The Constitution is the creation of the American political institution, not of the government. As new stories arise within the political institution, controversies and debates ensue. Some of these new stories require changes in the Constitution; some require changes in other laws and the enactment of new laws. The political stories associated with the historic developments known as abolitionism, woman suffrage, civil rights, the labor movement, free enterprise, and manifest destiny have all had great impact on the American constitutional-legal system.

Not all of the stories generated and disseminated by the American political institution achieve their effects through constitutional or legal action. Some political stories affect patterns of cooperative action through the creation of public opinion, that is, through the creation of attitudes instead of or in addition to legal obligations. The economic story that Americans identify as free enterprise creates myriad attitudes and values and is generated in many sectors of the political institution. These attitudes and values are as important to American economic life as capital and raw materials. The abolitionist, civil rights, woman suffrage, and other movements mentioned above all created attitudes that were essential to the success of these movements. Ultimately the attitudes created by stories are the prime movers of social life.

The political institution in the United States thus serves the same purpose as its counterparts elsewhere. It determines patterns of cooperative action by means of the stories it creates and disseminates. Political stories organize the life of a species that possesses no biochemical determinants of social behavior. Nonhuman social animals depend on biological systems to produce the patterns of cooperative action that sustain life in particular surroundings. Human beings depend on political stories.

LITERATURE 2

The stability and continuity of all animal life depends on the existence and functioning of fixed structures. Patterns of life are stable and continuous generation after generation because the systems that govern these patterns consist of fixed structures. In nonhuman animals the fixed structures are chemical. The genetic code is a stable code. The changes and adaptations that occur in animals whose lives and actions depend on the genetic code are limited to those that result from mutation and the recombinations, which are consequences of interbreeding.

The fixed structures that provide stability and continuity for human beings are not stable chemical structures; they are stable cultural structures. We call these stable cultural structures literature.

In common usage the word *literature* generally refers to imaginative writings, to belles lettres or criticisms thereof. We use the term in a much broader sense to refer to the special story units and collections upon which the entire story system of a culture depends. The literature of a culture is part of its story system, but it is the central part, the nucleus that controls the functions and development of the rest.

The essential characteristic that distinguishes the literature of a culture from the rest of its story system is fixed formulation. The literature of a culture consists of stories specially composed so as to be available verbatim throughout the culture and transmissible verbatim to succeeding generations.

Literature is composed and transmitted both orally and in writing. The oral method involves the composition and transmission techniques associated with epic poetry. In preliterate societies "the only possible verbal technology available to guarantee the preservation and fixity of transmission was that of the rhythmic word organized cunningly in verbal and metrical patterns which were unique enough to retain their shape. This is the historical genesis . . . the moving cause of that phenomenon we still call poetry."[1]

The technology that a culture uses to store and transmit its literature determines the culture's development. In a preliterate society the continuity of life depends on the oral transfer of the stories that support social life. The stories created within the culture cannot be transmitted from generation to generation if they are not fixed in literary formulae and passed from living memory to living memory. If the memorizers are killed, the literature does not survive and the culture does not survive. The Koran, a work of literature originally composed for oral transmission, was written down nineteen years after the death of Mohammed. It was put in writing because the memorizers were being killed in the battles that accompanied the spread of the faith. The importance that preliterate societies place on precision is illustrated by the reverence of the Moslems for the first official version of the Koran, the "first, final, and only canonized version."[2] All other Koranic texts were destroyed. The 6,239 verses, 77,934 words, and 323,621 letters of the official version were painstakingly counted. No authorized translation of the Koran exists except for an official Turkish version. The commitment of the Koran to writing ensured its survival. It is difficult to imagine what the course of world history would have been if the Koran had died with its memorizers in a skirmish in the seventh century.

The development of a preliterate culture is limited by the capacity of the human memory. The limited capacity of memory restricts the quantity of literature that can be preserved. Only the most essential stories are transferred from generation to generation. Little is added. Only those new stories that are of sufficient importance to be included with the essential traditions of the group are added to the burdens of the memorizers. When these burdens reach their limits, nothing more can be added unless something is displaced, forgotten, or lost.

With the invention of writing, the capacity of a culture to store and transmit literature is vastly enlarged, even to infinity.[3] Cultural development is freed from the bonds that tie it to the capacity of human memory and is limited only by human creativity. The single fact of literacy is what makes the last five thousand years of human history so different from the previous seventy thousand.

The literature of a culture, the nucleus of its story system, controls the story system as a whole. The evolution of a story system is directed by the literature. Developments in literature cause old stories to pass away and new stories to appear. New stories are never totally new. There is no such thing as absolute novelty, however original a creation may be. Even the most original story will betray its relationship to previously existing literature in some way. The life of a culture is determined more by its literature than by anything else. The most salient and characteristic features of a culture are created and sustained by its literature. Continuity depends on literature. All human beings, not just Jews, Christians, and Moslems, are "people of the book." The book may be oral or written, a simple saga or a voluminous scientific corpus; but it is always there. People who possessed no literature would possess no real world, no past, no institutions; they would not be recognizable as human.

Since the dawn of literacy, two types of literature have been preserved: the literature of knowledge and the literature of imagination. Whether or not the literature of imagination was preserved before the invention of writing is open to question.[4] But ever since the invention of writing led to the creation of new literary forms such as the drama and the novel, the literature of imagination has played an important role in the life of literate societies.

The basic distinction between the literature of knowledge and the literature of imagination is not easy to specify. One cannot distinguish them on the basis of relationships to "reality," by saying, for example, that the literature of knowledge deals with existing entities and phenomena and the literature of the imagination does not. All such attempts fail. The flowers that are the subject of a botanical essay are no more real than the flowers that are the subject of a poem. The nature of phenomena such as love and virtue can be presented with equal validity in a novel or in an ethical treatise. Furthermore, the entities that populate a work of pure mathematics are as imaginary as the characters in a drama. The practice of distinguishing persists, however, regardless of how difficult it may be to justify theoretically. Distinguishing science and history from poetry and fiction presents no problem in practice.

The theoretical basis for the distinction is not in the literature; it is in the audience. The classification of a work as literature of knowledge or literature of imagination depends on the views of the audience. Audiences make their judgments concerning particular works on the basis of cultural guidelines, which indicate the role that invention or imagination shall play in the creation of a work of literature. That is, audiences allow a certain role to invention or imagination in works of the literature of knowledge and a different role in works of the literature of imagination. When audiences classify a work as literature of knowledge rather than literature of imagination, it is because they judge that invention played the role appropriate to the former rather than the latter. For example, contemporary Western guidelines permit a historian to invent theories and explanations, but not characters or events. If an audience judges that an author claiming to be a historian has invented characters or events, the audience will reject his claim and classify his work as legend, myth, or historical fiction. Similarly, scientists may invent hypothetical entities such as quarks, and they may invent mathematical constructs; but they may not invent chemical properties or experimental results.

The story system of a culture provides the guidelines that audiences use to classify literature. The guidelines are primarily derived from the portions of the story system that specify or imply what is possible and what is not possible and the portions that specify or imply how reliable knowledge is acquired. Thus, an audience attempting to classify a report describing the parting of the Red Sea as literature of knowledge or literature of imagination will do so on the basis of whether or not they believe such a phenomenon is possible and, if so, how one might determine whether or not it occurred as reported. For some audiences the report of such an event in sacred scriptures would be sufficient evidence that the event occurred as reported and was not invented or imagined by the author. Other audiences would not accept such evidence, either because they believe the event reported to be impossible, or because they believe the event to be so unlikely as to render the unsubstantiated report useless as evidence. The latter audiences would regard the event as imagined or invented and classify the report as literature of imagination.

Works of literature classified as imaginative within the culture that produced them are generally accepted as such by other cultures. However, intercultural disagreements concerning works classified as literature of knowledge are common. In Moslem culture the *Koran* is classified as literature of knowledge; it is a revelation given by god to the Prophet. In Western cultures the *Koran* is generally classified as a work of the literature of imagination, as a work of poetry created by Mohammed. The *Koran* is so classified by Westerners, because its content is considered incompatible with the literature of knowledge that describes and explains reality for Westerners. Currently, Western stories of reality are based mostly on scientific literature. But even before scientific literature existed, Westerners rejected the *Koran* because of its incompatibility with Christian literature.

The rejection by one culture of the literature of knowledge of another is ultimately justified by experience. But as we indicated earlier in our discussion of story systems, experiences depend on stories of reality. In the following passage from one of Castaneda's works, a Westerner's knowledge and experience of a natural phenomenon encounter the knowledge and experience of a Yaqui Indian. The mutual incomprehension and frustration that result from conflicting literatures and conflicting experiences based on literature are clearly evident.

Castaneda and don Juan, a Yaqui Indian, are hiding from the wind in don Juan's house. Don Juan has told the incredulous Castaneda that the wind is angry, that it is better to stay indoors. Castaneda tells the old man that he cannot believe it and that the old man's view of the wind is incorrect.

> "What is the wind then?" [don Juan] asked in a challenging tone.
>
> I patiently explained to him that masses of hot and cold air produced different pressures and that the pressure made the masses of air move vertically and horizontally. It took me a long time to explain all the details of basic meteorology.
>
> "You mean that all there is to the wind is hot and cold air?" he asked in a tone of bafflement.
>
> "I'm afraid so," I said and silently enjoyed my triumph.

Don Juan seemed to be dumbfounded. But then he looked at me and began to laugh uproariously.

"Your opinions are final opinions," he said with a note of sarcasm. "They are the last word, aren't they? For a hunter, however, your opinions are pure crap. It makes no difference whether the pressure is one or two or ten; if you would live out here in the wilderness you would know that during the twilight the wind becomes power. A hunter that is worth his salt knows that and acts accordingly."[5]

Both the Westerner and the Yaqui have experienced the wind in terms of their own literature of knowledge. Each is astonished at the attitude of the other. Each appraises the "knowledge" of the other in disparaging terms—"rather simplistic," "pure crap"—the experience of each justifies his view.

The role of literature in culture gives particular importance to the role of communication professionals in social life. In every culture the relationship of literature to social life is strongly conditioned by communication professionals, whether they be poets, memorizers, preachers, printers, scribes, teachers, authors, singers, actors, librarians, broadcasters, or publishers. It is only through an understanding of the nature and function of literature that the role of the communication professional can be itself understood.

Since this book is directed mainly to American communication professionals, our discussion of literature will focus mainly on American literature. The principles that organize this discussion, however, are generally applicable.

LITERATURE OF KNOWLEDGE

The literature that is the foundation of the American story system is immense and diverse. Its origins go back to the dawn of literacy, to the writings of Ancient Greece and the Near East. These ancient literatures were the primary sources of European literature, and American literature is essentially an extension of European literature. The influence of two European literary traditions outweighs that of all others. These are the British philosophical-legal tradition and the European intellectual-scientific tradition. American political literature and the literature of the natural and social sciences are based on these traditions. These provide American social life with its most essential, prominent, and characteristic features.

The most important works of American literature are the Declaration of Independence and the Constitution. These works are unique in that they have served as the primary foundations of the American story system since the nation came into existence as a distinct social entity. Unlike the other literature that creates American life, they are not intercultural; they are specifically American. American social identity is based on them; the continuity of American history is provided by them. The Declaration and Constitution play a role in American culture comparable to the roles played by the *Old Testament, Talmud,* and *Midrash* in Jewish culture, the *Koran* in Moslem culture, and the works of Marx and Lenin in Soviet culture.

The Declaration of Independence and the Constitution determine the basic categories of American social life, the categories through which individuals and groups are related to one another and to the society as a whole. Americans can deal with social processes only in terms of the categories of these two works of literature. From the Great Debate of the late eighteenth century to the civil rights and women's rights controversy of the late twentieth century, the issues have been the same: reconciling the necessities of the state with the freedom of individuals, reconciling security and order with liberty, reconciling the rights of the majority with those of minorities, establishing and protecting the liberty of certain groups without infringing upon the liberty or compromising the equality of others. The history of American culture is primarily a history of the interpretation of the Declaration of Independence and of the interpretation and emendation of the Constitution.[6]

Scientific literature is not specifically American. The influence of scientific literature, though never absent, was not always as strong in American culture as it is today. Of its contemporary impact there can be no doubt. The literature of the natural and social sciences is second only to the Declaration and Constitution in its impact on the American story system.

The most important functions of the literature of the natural sciences in American culture are providing the story of the natural order and the story of knowledge. This does not mean that everyone in the culture believes the scientific story or even knows that it exists. It does mean that whenever state action relates in any way to a story of the cosmic order, the story that the state uses is the one contained in the literature of the natural sciences. For example, the state legislates the story of the cosmic order to be systematically taught in public schools; the one presently selected is the one contained in the literature of the natural sciences.

The story of the cosmic order in the literature of the natural sciences combines with the story of the human order in the Declaration of Independence to provide a type of religious unity for American culture. On the surface, American religion appears pluralistic. This is an illusion created by a misconception concerning the nature of religion. A religion is a system of descriptions and explanations, the most important of which deal with the nature of the universe and the nature of man. If people generally accept a way of life based on the same stories of the universe and of man, they share essentially the same religion. The way of life that Americans generally accept is based on a view of the universe created in the literature of the natural sciences and a view of man contained in the Declaration of Independence. These provide Americans with the religious unity essential to any culture.

In American culture it is the function of the literature of the natural sciences to distinguish the possible from the impossible, to indicate the nature of the earth and the substances it provides, and to specify the nature of the other life forms that share the environment. The economic life of the society is determined by such stories. They legitimize and support the activities most essential to American economic life: agriculture, mining, extracting fossil fuels, and harvesting timber.

These activities that sustain American life are impossible in the real world of some Native American groups. They live in a real world where the earth and natural objects are animate, personal, and sensate.

When we dig roots we make little holes. When we build houses we make little holes. We don't chop down trees. We use only dead wood. But the white people plow up the ground, pull down trees, kill everything. The tree says, "don't. I am sore. Don't hurt me." But they chop it down and cut it up. The spirit of the land hates them. They blast out trees and stir it up to its depths. They saw up the trees. That hurts them. The Indians never hurt anything, but the white people destroy all. They blast rocks and scatter them on the ground. The rock says, "don't. You are hurting me." But the white people pay no attention.[8]

The white people pay no attention because this world does not exist for them. In their real world the earth and rocks are inanimate and impersonal; trees are insensate. The only qualities that these entities possess are the qualities indicated in the literature of the natural sciences. Americans plow up the ground, cut the trees, and stir the land to its depths without regard to any offense that might be given. Logging and mining and agriculture are totally unaffected by concern about inflicting pain on rocks and trees or by concern about provoking the spirit of the land, because it is simply not possible to do any of these things. In the world described by the literature of the natural sciences, no such possibilities exist.

The other major contribution of the literature of the natural sciences to American culture is the story of knowledge that it provides. The religious literature of a culture provides instructions or prescriptions for achieving truth and avoiding error. In American society the literature of the sciences performs this function.

The scientific story of knowledge says that in order to learn the truth about reality, one must observe it without preconception, see what it does, formulate general propositions on the basis of observations, and test these propositions by experimentation. True statements are statements confirmed by experiments, statements that enable the prediction of experimental results, and statements that can be rigorously deduced therefrom.[9] In American culture knowledge is generally identified with scientific knowledge.

In recent years, however, doubts concerning this story of knowledge have been expressed in some of the literature of the most mature of the sciences, physics. First, some contemporary physicists maintain that one cannot simply go out and observe phenomena and, after observation, take the steps that produce a theory. One must have a theory before one begins observation. Aspects of nature can be selected for observation only on the basis of a theory. As Einstein said, "it is the theory which decides what can be observed."[10] One does not seek to observe phenomena whose occurrence one does not suspect. No one sought data concerning the earth's orbit before Copernicus, because no one suspected that the earth was a planet. Prior to 1770, one could not observe or report upon the phenomenon *oxidation*; prior to 1895, one could not gather data concerning the behavior of X rays; prior to 1963, no one sought to observe the behavior of quarks. Reports of observations are always reports based on assumptions about the nature of things, which directed the search for data in the first place. And these reports are formulated in the vocabulary and concepts that the historic state of his discipline makes available to the observer.[11]

Other doubts raised by contemporary scientists concern methods of observation and testing, or experiments. The generally accepted view of scientific investigation supposes that it is possible to isolate the observer from the phenomenon being observed. The generally accepted view assumes that what the observer sees is a phenomenon produced by nature. Physicists now believe, however, that the process of scientific investigation disrupts the systems under observation. The impact of the process of investigation upon experimental results will depend upon the sensitivity of the observed system to the investigative procedures used.

> Conventional notions of scientific investigation are based on the assumption that we study nature as it "really is." We imagine a world which exists in space and time and follows its natural laws, independent of any observing subject. . . . When we produce new phenomena by means of our experimental equipment, we are convinced that we do not really produce new phenomena: that is, we believe that actually these phenomena occur frequently in nature without our interference, and our equipment is just made to isolate and to study them. . . .
>
> But are we really entitled to do so?[12]

Some scientists now say that things are not so simple. The observer can seek only those phenomena that are rendered accessible by his theoretical approach. He can report his observations only in the language and concepts made available by a historically determined discipline. The instruments and techniques of observation will affect his findings to the degree that the objects of observation are sensitive to these instruments and techniques. A leading historian of science, Thomas S. Kuhn, states that the new concept of knowledge created by twentieth-century physics must change our notion of scientific progress.

A scientific theory is usually felt to be better than its predecessors not only in the sense that it is a better instrument for discovering and solving puzzles but also because it is somehow a better representation of what nature is really like. One often hears that successive theories grow ever closer to, or approximate more and more closely to, the truth. Apparently generalizations like that refer . . . to the match . . . between the entities with which the theory populates nature and what is "really there."

Perhaps there is some other way of salvaging the notion of "truth" for application to whole theories, but this one will not do. There is, I think, no theory-independent way to reconstruct phrases like "really there"; the notion of a match between the ontology of a theory and its "real" counterpart in nature now seems to me illusive in principle.[13]

What Kuhn is saying is that however effective an instrument science is for problem solving and for concrete predictions, it cannot tell us how things "really are," and the ability to solve problems and to make predictions should not be confused with the ability to discover how things really are.

Einstein and Infeld said essentially the same thing:

In our endeavor to understand reality we are somewhat like a man trying to understand the mechanism of a closed watch. He sees the face and the moving hands, even hears its ticking, but he has no way of opening the case. If he is ingenious he may form some picture of a mechanism which could be responsible for all the things he observes, but he may never be quite sure that his picture is the only one which could explain his observations. He will never be able to compare his picture with the real mechanism and he cannot even imagine the possibility or the meaning of such a comparison.[14]

The new story of knowledge created in physics does not unduly disrupt the agenda of what Kuhn calls "normal science." Normal science is devoted to problem solving and concrete prediction, and these activities can continue even as natural scientists abandon hope of discovering how things really are.

It is not yet possible to say what effect the new story of knowledge will have on American society. Since the seventeenth century, science has overcome every rival system that opposed its claim to possessing the key to truth. Now in the twentieth century, with its competitors all but destroyed by its attacks, science, represented by the physicists, has renounced its own claim. It remains to be seen what the ultimate effect will be.

The social sciences were created in Western Europe in the eighteenth century. The impulse came from the natural sciences. Newtonian physics gave birth to the story that the universe is an orderly system in all of its parts, that the laws of nature regulate the behavior of everything that exists. Man and his institutions are not exceptional; they too are subject to the laws of nature. The "discovery" of the laws that regulate human action was to be the object of the new science of man and society.

From the very beginning, the new science of man and society played an important role in American life. The Declaration of Independence, which created the new nation, derived its basic principles from the law of nature. The Constitution created a structure designed to secure natural human rights. The great controversy between Hamilton and Jefferson was, in part, a confrontation of the ideas of the European economists François Quesnay and Adam Smith. Hamilton "read Adam Smith with eagerness and *The Wealth of Nations* was a source book for many of his state papers."[15] Jefferson "had read much in the works of the physiocrat group . . . the major principles of the school sank deep in his mind and creatively determined his thinking."[16] The *laissez-faire* spirit of nineteenth-century America was created, guided, and justified by a generation of European economic literature.

As the other social sciences developed, they exercised a powerful influence on American life. *Laissez-faire* economic and social doctrines overlaid with the social Darwinism of Herbert Spencer and William Graham Sumner produced the widely accepted story that society was an arena in which natural evolutionary forces should be permitted to exercise their regulatory power without interference. Planning and legislative programs were stigmatized as meddling with natural laws, which, if left to do their work, would fashion the optimum social order by selecting the fit and eliminating the unfit.

The social havoc created by the orthodox *laissez-faire* story and social Darwinism led to the creation of a counter story near the end of the century. A leading creator and exponent of the counter story was Lester Frank Ward (1841-1913), "the father of American sociology."

Ward's story was built on faith in the social sciences. He believed that social science gave man the power to direct the forces of evolution. He believed that social progress could not be achieved by *laissez faire*.

> True liberty could flourish only where the state interposed itself between the strong and the weak, the privileged and the unprivileged, the cunning and the simple, and where it undertook to establish equality of opportunity and of bargaining power, insure economic security, and lift up the general level of intelligence. All this could be achieved by wise legislation.[17]

For almost a hundred years the competing stories of William Graham Sumner and Lester Frank Ward have been the basis for the great social struggles in America. The principles they represented inspired the ideological struggles between the champions of free silver and sound money, private enterprise and government control, rugged individualism and the welfare state. The principles of Sumner and Ward "were the basic issues of the Populist crusade, the progressive movement, the New Freedom, and most heatedly of all, the New Deal and the Fair Deal."[18] The controversy continues into the present. It is common today to hear their doctrines faithfully paraphrased by people who never heard of either of them.[19] Ward wholeheartedly believed that legislators should be social scientists. "No legislator is qualified to vote on or propose measures . . . until he masters all that is known of the science of society. Every true legislator must be a sociologist."[20] Legislators have responded to Ward's prescription, not by becoming social scientists themselves, but by believing in social science and by directing their activities in accordance with information created by social scientists. At the present time in the United States, there is no authoritative source of information dealing with man and society other than the social sciences. The social sciences are now all-encompassing.

No sources other than the social sciences have any official standing in American culture. All social programs are based on information generated in the literature of the social sciences. Decisions affecting economics, education, law enforcement, cities, families, minorities, the old and the young, the mentally and the socially infirm depend on the social sciences. In public schools the only stories systematically told about man and society are those presented in "social studies." Economists, demographers, sociologists, counselors, psychologists, educators, criminologists, statisticians, social workers, public administrators, and ethnologists now constitute a multitude whose activities intersect with the life of every American. The position attained by the social sciences in the United States at present would probably exceed the most optimistic hopes of Lester Frank Ward. It is now possible for Americans to conduct every significant aspect of life on the basis of information contained in the literature of the social sciences. The entire life cycle is covered. Elizabeth Kubler-Ross and others have recently incorporated the counseling and consoling of the dying.

The social sciences have always been sensitive to major developments in the natural sciences. The natural law story of the eighteenth century played a central role in their creation. The Darwinian story of the nineteenth century played a central role in their development. The authority of social science was, from the very beginning, borrowed from natural science. The story of human nature and human institutions that was created in the literature of the social sciences was accepted because it was guaranteed by the methodology of the natural sciences. There can be no doubt that the new story of knowledge created in twentieth-century physics will ultimately have great impact on the social sciences. If the natural sciences surrender their claim to yield truth, the social sciences can do no less.

Before the new story of knowledge arrived on the scene, it was generally believed that the natural and social sciences possessed the means to discover the objective truth about reality. It was believed that the history of science recorded its progress in discovering this truth. As these beliefs are abandoned, it becomes necessary to reinterpret the history of the natural and social sciences. If the natural and social sciences have not been discovering the nature of reality for the past two or three hundred years, what have they been doing?

The natural sciences, Kuhn would say, have always done what they do now, that is, solve puzzles and work out problems of prediction. The value of a particular scientific acomplishment depends upon its utility as an instrument for discovering and solving puzzles and making concrete predictions. The social sciences, however, have never been involved in such puzzle-solving and predictions. The social sciences, from the very beginning, have been involved in the common human activity of creating reality through literature.

A crucial, if unarticulated, assumption of the scientific method is that the literature that scientific activity generates does not affect the behavior of objects of investigation. This assumption, however, is valid only for natural science. No one has ever maintained that the behavior of metals or acids is affected in any way by what is written about them in literature. If the behavior of natural objects were affected by what literary traditions say about them, natural science would be impossible. It is clear, however, that the behavior of men and institutions is more affected by what literature says than by anything else. No factor plays a greater role in shaping human behavior than literature, including the literature of the social sciences. For the past two hundred years, the social sciences have been creating and shaping human behavior and institutions through the very literature that claimed to describe and explain them. For the past two hundred years, the theories and explanations of economists, psychologists, educators, and other social scientists have been producing and shaping human behavior and social structures as effectively as the writings of poets and theologians ever did.[21]

It appears that science has one last shock to administer to the religious sensibilities of Western man. Science asserts that the scientific critique, the instrument that destroyed the confidence of Western man in divinely revealed truth, must now destroy the confidence of Western man in science. If ancient religions could not reveal the objective truth about god, nature, and man, neither can science. The era of objective truth is nearly over in the West.

LITERATURE OF IMAGINATION

The literature of imagination is literature that is designated as such by audiences. The designation of a work as literature of imagination means that, in the judgment of the audience, the role of invention was essentially unrestricted.

The literature of imagination plays an important role in American culture. The dominant forms are poetry, drama, and fiction. The scale of distribution is immense. The role of this literature in education and as the staple of the broadcasting industry ensures that it will reach a huge audience. Printed fiction, cinematic and televised drama, and recorded popular songs have a daily audience of tens of millions of people. The function of the literature of imagination is to provide experience and insight; its ability to do so is the basis for its great popularity and for its importance in social life.

The experience that the literature of imagination provides is vicarious experience. Vicarious experience is experience-at-a-distance; it is the experience of an observer. Vicarious experience produces in the bodies of observers the physical responses that observers have learned to associate with actual experiences, the physical responses that they would anticipate if they were actually involved in what they observe. Depending on the action or situation observed, the observer may undergo changes in heart rate, blood pressure, and respiration; he may perspire, weep, become sexually excited; he may experience nervous or muscular tension, nausea, the emotions of sorrow, joy, exhilaration, revulsion.

The observer must somehow enter into the action or situation in order to undergo the experience. There are two modes of entry. One is identification, establishing personal empathy with characters in the observed action or situation. The other is self-projection, transferring the self into observed actions or situations in which no characters are present or without making identification with characters that are present.

The capacity for identification and self-projection differs widely. There are many bases for the differences, for example, culture, sex, age, education. Many Americans cannot identify with the characters in a Medieval morality play; young children cannot project themselves into erotic situations. People with certain levels of education and intelligence may find it difficult to identify with complex and obscure characters like Hamlet, Ahab, or Oedipus. Many adults cannot identify with the characters in children's stories. The types of literature of imagination that provide vicarious experience to the widest audiences are those that offer minimal obstacles to identification and self-projection, the types that present characters and situations that are accessible to many classes of persons.

Ease of identification and self-projection accounts for the standard character types and situations in literature. Literature is replete with heroes, heroines, love, danger, violence, conflict, and crisis because most human beings respond to these. Human nature and the ordinary course of human existence are such that all human beings are highly susceptible to these characters and situations.

The drive that impels people to seek vicarious experience is far stronger than is generally realized or acknowledged. It is this drive that sustains the enormous industries that distribute the literature of imagination and that gathers tens of thousands of people to hear a singer and tens of millions to watch a television drama. The audiences gather day after day, year after year. It does not matter if the presentations they witness are only marginally different from one another. Their power to attract does not depend on novelty or variety.

The range and depth of human susceptibility to vicarious experience, the power of the impulse to seek it, and the unsavory character of some of the works that provide it often make people uncomfortable. The enjoyment of vicarious experience is stigmatized as childish, escapist, or even morbid. It is true, as we shall see, that some works produced to exploit the hunger for vicarious experience can be detrimental both to the individual and to society. It should be realized, however, that the capacity for vicarious experience is a human capability of the utmost value. Vicarious experience enables human beings to extend their experience in space and time without limit. The power of literature to provide vicarious experience is one of the qualities that makes literature so important in individual and social life. Literature preserves experience and provides the observer's vantage point. Without the vicarious experience that literature provides, the range and variety of experiences available to the individual would be drastically and deplorably reduced. Human psychic and social life would be radically impoverished.

Another benefit the literature of imagination provides is insight. We use the term *insight* to refer to a particular intellectual mode. Distinguishing insight as an intellectual mode is ancient and persistent. Men have always appreciated the difference between learning and wisdom, between intelligence and judgment, between seeing or hearing and understanding. Wisdom, judgment, and understanding are all types of insight. Insight is comprehensive and balanced discernment that grasps essential factors in their proper relationships. The objects of intellectual modes other than insight are matters of fact, quantity, objective descriptions, measurements, and the like. The objects of insight are significance, value, meaning, quality, and the like.

The objects of insight are generally complex and abstract; they are not tangible nor easily discerned. They are hidden beneath appearances and within complexity; they are obscured by ordinary ways of seeing and knowing, concealed by the conventional and familiar, pushed aside by everyday events and concerns. Insight is never facile.

At the same time, insight is neither rare nor mystical. The discernment of beauty and excellence and nobility are all acts of insight; so also are the acts that grasp their antitheses: squalor, baseness, and meanness. All people are capable of discerning these things.

The catalyst of insight is experience. This is why wisdom, judgment, and understanding are rare in the very young and naive. Experience teaches people respect for the complexities and ambiguities of human existence. It enables them to learn the difference between the ephemeral and the durable, to learn what hides behind appearances, to know the long-term consequences of values and decisions, to feel the effects of long-term patterns of action. Experience is the solvent of obliviousness.

The literature of imagination teaches by experience. The concepts of significance, meaning, and value, which are created in it, are communicated to the audience by drawing the audience into the context of life that a work presents. Once involved, the attitude of the audience is no longer objective or purely cognitive. Members of the audience respond to the work as they respond to actual life experience. The whole person is involved in the response. Body, mind, and emotions react as the individual lives another life in the world created by the author. This learning experience is radically different from a purely cognitive experience.

According to Eric Havelock, it was this type of learning experience provided by poetry that prompted Plato to attack it in *The Republic.* Plato regarded poetry as a kind of psychic poison and as the enemy of truth[22] because of the way it teaches. Poetry captivates, seduces, casts a spell, hypnotizes, overpowers. Reason sleeps, logic ceases, as the audience is swept away. How can one sustain the rational and objective attitude that leads to knowledge when one is in the state aroused by poetry? One should be instructed in courage and wisdom by means of principles, not by means of the engrossing experience of identification with Achilles, Odysseus, and Nestor.[23] Poetry and poets were not welcome in the republic.

As one of the first rationalist teachers, Plato was well aware of the difference between learning from principles and learning from vicarious experience. His attack on poetry is testimony to the power of literature of imagination.

It is the ability of the literature of imagination to provide experience that enables it to provide insight. If this literature can lead men astray, it can also lead to wisdom and understanding. The poet, dramatist, and novelist can communicate his message concerning matters of significance, value, and meaning with fullness, clarity, and force because he can transport his audience into a context of life in which the audience learns not from principle but from experience. Thus, the understanding that Melville offers concerning the human condition requires that his audiences go on a whaling voyage and live in another world. From this world they should return not schooled in principles but changed by experience. The experience is essential. One cannot receive the value of *Moby Dick* from a summary. The novel is not replaceable by the treatise.

Insight is the pinnacle and grace of intelligence. Human beings without wisdom and judgment and understanding, who are oblivious to the complexities and ambiguities of life, who know only what seems or what is on the surface, who are insensitive to quality, are personally deficient and socially incompetent. This is why the literature of imagination has such great social importance. It is the type of literature that, more than any other, is capable of humanizing and socializing intelligence.

The literature of imagination has played an important role in creating social reality in American culture. One form in particular, the novel, has had an especially powerful effect. The English and American novel of the eighteenth and nineteenth centuries created both the basis for marriage and the story of femininity that are prevalent in American culture.

The English society of the eighteenth century that produced the novel was in the later stages of reorganization on the basis of the humanist, protestant, and rationalist story traditions that had superseded the Medieval tradition. The new stories of human nature and human activity, the new values and ideals created since the Renaissance, were visible in the development of the modern parliamentary system, the new status and power of wealth and of the middle class, and the transformation of England into a commercial and industrial nation. The process begun in the sixteenth century was nearing completion by the middle of the eighteenth.

While England was an agrarian society, the country's marriage customs and attitudes toward women were based on the old story tradition. Young people married when the adults responsible for them decided they should, and they married the persons chosen for them by their families. In an agrarian society, marriage means the incorporation of a new family member. The adults sought to exclude any who might disrupt the household or add to its burdens through ill health, ill temper, or laziness. Marriage was a family business and not a matter to be left to the couple, who were often quite young when the marriage decision was made. The adults who selected one individual over another often did so in order to secure some sort of advantage for the family. The existence of a personal-sexual attraction between the young people, a mutual attraction which we call "being in love," had nothing whatever to do with marriage. The status of women was low both legally and socially. English law reflected the grossly inferior status of women. The children of a marriage were the husband's; only the husband could sue for divorce; the husband had the right to punish his wife by beating her or having her imprisoned.[24]

In twentieth-century England and the United States no vestige of the old marriage system remains. Marriages are no longer arranged by families; the decision belongs to the couple. The only respectacle basis for marriage is the personal-sexual attraction known as "being in love." The social and legal status of women and attitudes toward women have changed considerably.

All of these changes are related to the development of the novel. Romantic love as a basis for marriage was invented in the novel. The romantic novel produced and disseminated the story of femininity that was accepted without question in the United States until very recently and is still very much in evidence. The paradigm was created by Samuel Richardson;[25] its essential elements were as follows: Women are not to be regarded as simply inferior to men; they are different from men. Like Clarissa Harlowe, they are naturally possessed of qualities of moral and spiritual excellence that make them, in some ways, superior to men, who are basically coarse and lustful and inclined to exploit women sexually. It is not right to force a woman to marry any man. To do so is to make her submit to an assault on her purity and delicacy. Woman's nature is such that sexual relations are only to be endured if they involve a man to whom she has freely given her love, a love that includes no sexual passion or lust. Its object is a man, but its qualities are benevolence, charity, generosity. Any physical concomitants are a concession to male animality and to the whim of nature that has made children the issue of this unsavory carnality. To force a woman to submit to sex is an unspeakable crime; as Pamela says, "to rob a person of her virtue is worse than cutting her throat." A woman may, however, submit to sex in a marriage based on love. Initially, the man is heedless of love and pursues the woman determined to have "his way with her." The woman resists his seductive and oppressive designs, attempting all the while to purify his impulses by the force of her virtue and regenerative affection. She cares for him in spite of his moral primitivism. But unless he accepts her view of love and marriage, she will not give herself. She would rather die or live in seclusion echoing Pamela: "May I never survive, one moment, that fatal one in which I shall forfeit my innocence." Gradually, the man comes around. He perceives the splendid qualities of the woman: her purity, temperance, refinement, delicacy, modesty, spirituality. He begins to realize his own unworthiness. He finds, one day, that he has no wish but to match her eternal devotion with his own. His sexual passion purged by virtuous example has become chaste; the purity he once sought to corrupt he would now protect with his life. They marry knowing their union was destined by heaven, knowing that their wedding is the central and transcendent event of their lives. They will be happy ever after.

The basis for marriage created in the romantic novel became the basis for marriage in American society. The model of femininity created in the novel became the standard American model. Americans married those with whom they "fell in love." American women embodied, aspired to, and trained their daughters in the model of femininity created in the novel. The attitude toward sex that the novel prescribed captured the American psyche and has only recently begun to release its grip.

The chaste romantic love that the novel presented as the only respectable basis for marriage is erotic passion with the sexual origins and elements denied or obscured. When romantic love is concerned, all the accompaniments of erotic passion are allowed except one, sex, which is placed in opposition to the rest. The psychological conflicts that resulted gave rise to the attitude toward sex that we call Victorian.

The ancients were familiar with erotic passion. The well-known syndrome appears in ancient scripture and tragedy, which present erotic passion as carnal, obsessive violent, jealous, demanding, distracting, delusive, consuming. The ancients did not regard this state as noble or excellent. A man or woman in the grip of this passion was quite likely to do something foolish or worse. David and Samson, consumed by passion, did criminal and disgraceful deeds. Phaedra in an erotic fury lost her mind and her life. In erotic passion there is danger of tragic madness; the ancients prayed that the gods would protect them from this infirmity.[26] Such a state, of course, had nothing to do with marriage.

In the Middle Ages the status of erotic passion was drastically changed. The troubadour poets of eleventh-century France transformed erotic passion into courtly love. In their poetry it was asserted, for the first time, that "love between the sexes is to be regarded as the supreme value of life on earth."[27] No longer was a man or woman stricken with passion an object of ridicule or pity. In troubadour poetry, passion became noble and excellent and raised life to a higher plane. Though passion might still be tragic, it was also glorious. The troubadour poetry was clear about one thing, however. Courtly love had nothing to do with marriage. Indeed, this love was adulterous love, incompatible with marriage.

By another transformation the erotic passion of the ancients and the courtly love of the troubadours became the romantic love of the novel. In the novel, people "fell in love." They exhibited most of the symptoms of erotic passion and courtly love. They were obsessed, distracted, jealous, deluded, consumed, but their love was, ultimately, not carnal; the sexual element was denied, suppressed, obscured. The existence of the excited and confused state known as "being in love," a state of erotic passion with its driving force unknown or unacknowledged, was the only acceptable reason for marrying. Marriage for other reasons, for advantageous alliance, property, heirs, for any practical purpose, became disgraceful. The psychosocial revolution thus accomplished bears witness to the power of literature in general and of the novel in particular.

According to Denis de Rougement, romantic love has had a most unfortunate impact on marriage and, consequently, on society at large.[28] If the novel is mostly to blame and if, in addition, it has contributed to the captivity of women by Victorian stereotypes and to the hatred and fear of sex, then the Platonic position on poetry no longer seems so alarmist or puzzling. The embarrassment that Plato's strictures on poetry have caused humanists and scholars has always been rooted in a conviction that poetry could hardly do much damage, or, for that matter, much good either. After all, they say, poetry is not what makes men act. The history of the rise and influence of the novel says otherwise.

The literature of imagination consists of two types: literature of art and literature of entertainment. The two are distinguished by their different capacities to provide the benefits of the literature of imagination: vicarious experience and insight. Literature of art provides both vicarious experience and insight; literature of entertainment provides only vicarious experience. Both of these literatures play important roles in American life.

The function of the literature of art is to provide insight. The literary artist is the author whose powers of perception, intellect, and expression enable him to indicate significance, meaning, and value in works of imaginative literature.

The statement that an artist seeks to communicate never consists of a set of propositions that might be communicated in an essay. A drama, novel, or poem that is a work of art cannot be reduced to a set of observations, premises, and conclusions. Involvement in a work of art is not like hearing a lecture or reading a treatise; it is like a term of existence in another life. Through art, audiences have access to multiple lives and to the enlarged understanding that multiple lives would make possible.

Suppose a person wished to gain an understanding of sin, penitence, hypocrisy, authentic religion, forgiveness, and vengeance. Such a person might read tracts on ethics, moral theology, and psychology, or he might read Hawthorne's *The Scarlet Letter*. In either case the subject is the same, but the learning experience is very different. With the tracts the emphasis is on cognition; with the novel the emphasis is on experience.

The Scarlet Letter situates the reader in another time and place and allows him to live other lives. In a specific situation the reader experiences sin, penitence, vengeance, and the rest through characters he both observes and identifies with. The reader participates in the emotions, conflicts, designs, and actions of his alter egos. The reader feels the pain of the social isolation that

Hester endures in pride without rancor; he feels the strength that love and generosity give her. He feels and comes to know intimately the frustration and agony of Dimmesdale's weakness and hypocrisy and unconfessed guilt; he knows, as if it were a part of his own life, the ugliness of Chillingworth's obsession with vengeance and the deadliness of the failure to understand and forgive. The novel provides what tracts can never provide: the opportunity to live through a set of authentic experiences designed to reveal every dimension and nuance of its subject with forcefulness and clarity. The result is a fullness of enlightenment and certitude that is simply not available from a treatise.

Not all works of art have the qualities of *The Scarlet Letter.* Hawthorne's work deals with basic human concerns without neglecting a single significant factor. His artistic skill produced a work capable of crossing barriers of space and time to reach audiences very different from the one to which the work was originally directed. Not all works can do this. But a work need not have all the qualities of *The Scarlet Letter* in order to qualify as a work of art. The essential thing about a work of art is that it offer authentic revelatory experience. The work need not be broad in scope; it need not be accessible to audiences far removed from it in space and time. All that is necessary is that the experience a work offers be adequate to life in richness, complexity, and authenticity. A work that offers experiences that misrepresent, distort, oversimplify, or lead to false expectations of life, or a work that offers experiences that life cannot offer, is not a work of art.

Many works of literature having no special standing with critics are works of art, that is, they offer significant and authentic revelatory experience. A work by a contemporary American novelist, George Higgins, provides a useful example, *The Friends of Eddie Coyle.* This book is not likely to find its way into literature courses; yet it is clearly a work of art. The subject of Higgins's novel is life in the lower echelons of the Boston underworld. Reading it provides an experience of that life with unmistakable authenticity. The impression of chaos and futility and moral imbecility, of stupid mercenary sordidness, has the ring of truth that is altogether foreign to the standard crime story in print or on film or on television. A side-by-side reading of Higgins and Mickey Spillane quickly reveals the difference between art and nonart. The same effect might be achieved by comparing a work like *The Spy Who Came In From the Cold* with a standard Ian Fleming thriller.

Art is not rare. Many books, films, and a few television dramas are works of art. They differ in scope, that is, in breadth and depth, of subject matter. They differ in generality, that is, in how adequately they make experience accessible across barriers of space and time. But a work of art need not treat a great subject in universal terms. All that is necessary is that it offer its audience significant time in another life.

Literature of entertainment, like art, provides vicarious experience; but unlike art, entertainment does not provide insight. The vicarious experience that entertainment provides does not yield wisdom or understanding. The experience that entertainment provides is an end in itself; it is sought for pleasure, diversion, satisfaction. Art is judged by its capacity to provide wisdom and understanding through vicarious experience; entertainment is judged by its capacity to provide vicarious experience that is satisfying in itself. Art enlightens; entertainment pleases.

The most popular forms of literature of entertainment in American culture are the novel, the drama—particularly cinematic and televised drama—and the popular song. They have a daily audience of tens of millions.

The standard offerings of entertainments are the experiences that the ordinary course of human existence renders most compelling, rare, or exciting. The limitations that culture and circumstances impose on individual experience are thus partly compensated in entertainments.[29] Love, sex, heroism, danger, adventure, conflict, the extraordinary or most exciting of experiences are the staples of entertainment. Through entertainment one can extend one's experience in space and time; one can participate in actions and situations that are dangerous, illegal, immoral, or impossible by reason of age, weakness, fear, or other physical or psychic insufficiency, and one can do so easily, repeatedly, and without real consequences. Virtually any experience of which one can conceive can be made available in entertainment. Though many of the experiences that entertainments offer are fantastic or inauthentic, they are, nevertheless, stimulating, enjoyable, satisfying, and important.

The value and importance of entertainment is generally underestimated. Literature that provides experience is regarded as frivolous in comparison to literature that provides knowledge or insight. Entertainment is considered unworthy of study or analysis, and there is little appreciation or understanding of its effects on individuals or society. It is not realized that entertainment has great value and social importance, that it changes life through the experience it provides, and that like the other types of literature it plays a role in fashioning the "real world" of its audience.

Entertainment enters into the creation of the real world of its audience in several different ways. One of these is inculcation and reinforcement by presupposition. The fantastic situations and events of entertainments occur in authentic physical and cultural settings, with the real world of common sense as background. The most outrageously unrealistic crime story, for example, is set in a contemporary city. The crime committed is really a crime. The operation of American laws, judicial institutions, values, attitudes toward crime and punishment, police organization, procedures, technology, and a host of other factors are taken for granted. The most fantastic criminal caught by the most impossible policemen is read his rights. The factors taken for granted are more numerous than those that are explicitly presented. The "real world" is thus continuously affirmed, reinforced, and inculcated in innumerable entertainments of all kinds; fables and fantasies are set in the landscape of the culture's real world and help to establish it as the world that exists.

Entertainment also disseminates and universalizes conventions and stereotypes. Conventional values and models are inserted into all kinds of settings and situations and are strongly affirmed as a consequence. An outer-space drama set in the distant future, like *Star Trek*, and a Western set in the last century, like *Gunsmoke*, both present heroes with essentially the same character, virtues, and attitudes. The star-ship captain and the town marshal are aggressive, decent, noble, courageous, and tolerant but conservative according to the same pattern. Marshal Dillon and Captain Kirk could easily fill the other's post. Their qualities span the eons and light years that separate them. The heroic stereotype is thus universalized by implication; the heroic qualities portrayed are affirmed as virtual absolutes.

In addition to reinforcing conceptions of reality that originate in other sources, entertainment also creates reality. People commonly use information from literature of entertainment as though it were literature of knowledge. This happens when the information presented in entertainments does not conflict with information derived from experience or from other types of literature. Children are, therefore, especially susceptible to entertainment; their experience and contact with literature are so limited that even the most fantastic presentations are accepted as realistic. Children are not, however, alone in their susceptibility to entertainment. Adults also accept some of the presentations of entertainment as representations of the real world if they possess no information that supports alternative views. Entertainment is thus an effective instrument of propaganda only when the conceptions it seeks to impose receive no competition from other sources.

The literature of entertainment has often played an important role in creating reality in American culture. In the 1850s the picture of slavery, of Southern plantation life, and of the characteristics of Black slaves presented in *Uncle Tom's Cabin* was widely accepted as realistic and had a powerful impact on people. The status of slavery as a moral issue in the North was significantly affected by the novel. When Harriet Beecher Stowe called on Abraham Lincoln during the Civil War he greeted her with the question, "Is this the little woman whose book made such a great war?" Insofar as the North's resolve to fight was based on a response of moral outrage to slavery, the question was appropriate.[30]

Uncle Tom's Cabin was also widely read overseas. It was translated into more than forty languages and dialects; forty pirated editions appeared in Great Britain and the colonies within a year of publication. In Germany, France, and England popular dramas based on the novel enjoyed large audiences; in December 1852, six London theaters presented Uncle Tom plays at the same time. Over half a million British women signed an address on slavery, which was sent to Mrs. Stowe. Small contributions to the antislavery cause sent from Scotland totaled one thousand pounds.[31] Foreigners had little information to oppose the realities of life in the South as presented by the Boston novelist.

The same kind of response to entertainment has occurred many times on a smaller scale. Half a century after Uncle Tom, the public response to Upton Sinclair's *The Jungle*, a novel depicting the appalling conditions in meat-packing plants, is generally acknowledged to have aided passage of the Pure Food and Drug Act in 1906. During World War II, the conception of the Japanese character that many Americans formed was based on the cruel, fanatical stereotype presented in Hollywood films. Recently, marine conservationists have expressed concern that the public response to *Jaws*, a motion picture about sharks, might lead to the promiscuous killing of those animals. And finally, for generations of Americans, the realities of frontier history and American Indian life have been those created in Western novels and films.

Literature of entertainment performs another important social function. It plays an important role in affective education; that is, it provides training in the production, development, organization, and expression of emotional responses. Human beings in general exhibit the same capacities for certain emotional states, for feelings of fear, joy, pity, sorrow, hatred, sexual passion, insecurity, triumph, pride, hostility. The stimuli that elicit these emotional states, however, are different in different cultures. What produces fear in some cultures does not produce it in others; what makes some people feel pity makes others feel contempt or hostility. The affective response a given stimulus elicits is always partly learned and is subject to change and reinforcement.

Entertainment provides experience, which produces emotional responses. It enables people to share the emotional states of characters with whom they have identified. The response of the character is the response of the audience. The stimulus that affects the character affects the audience. People learn to respond to life as they have responded to vicarious life in entertainments. Children learn from entertainment to fear ghosts and certain animals—gorillas, for example. Adults learn to direct and reinforce emotions of hatred and fear of a national enemy by participating in entertainment in which the enemy is cruel and vicious. Conventional emotional responses to beauty, money, power, and virtue are learned and reinforced.

Entertainment also conditions audiences to associate affective states with certain modes of expression. Audiences learn how to express intense emotion; they learn which kinds of acts are natural, appropriate, or desirable expressions of emotional states;

Audiences learn that fear makes women faint or cry; they learn that men give expression to pride and ambition through aggressive behavior, but women do not; they learn that violence is a natural expression of frustration or anger.

The most important role that entertainment plays in American culture is one it has played for generations. Entertainment is the primary source of cognitive and affective training in romantic love, that variety of sexual passion which, in American culture, leads to marriage. Entertainments provide information about and experience of romantic love to tens of millions of people daily in popular songs, novels, motion pictures, comics, magazines, and television dramas. From these sources people learn the fashions, conventions, language, and etiquette of love, the modes of expression appropriate for the various stages of love's development, techniques for dealing with the various problems and pitfalls of love such as competition, jealousy, rejection, opposition from parents. The innumerable aspects of love are analyzed and explored in entertainments in which virtually everyone participates. Americans learn that romantic love is a supreme value, especially for women. They learn that if people fall in love, it is natural and desirable that they should marry. They also learn that if people are not in love, they should not marry. Entertainment is a major factor in sustaining the marriage customs and sexual attitudes of the culture.

This chapter has dealt with the relationship of literature to culture. The conventional view of literature regards it as a product of culture. Culture exists and produces literature as a kind of artifact, important and influential to be sure, but nevertheless a product. The conventional view of literature sees it as a reflection or expression of life and action, as though life and action were somehow antecedent to literature, as if human beings had direct and unmediated contact with reality, which serves as the basis for literature. The conventional view is untenable. It fails in the face of human variety. It cannot account for the multiplicity of real worlds inhabited by human beings. But the variety and mutability of reality correspond to the variety and mutability of literature. Every aspect of reality and every change it exhibits can be traced to its source in literature. *Literature is not the product of culture; culture is the product of literature.*

COMMUNICATION 3
INDUSTRIES
IN AMERICA

Up to this point we have described and analyzed the components of the communication system that sustains human life: the system that enables human beings to create patterns of life and action, to adapt these patterns, and to transmit them from generation to generation. Language creates human intelligence and makes human cooperation possible. Story systems create the real world, the locus of group life. The major social institutions determine that particular stories of the cosmic and natural orders, stories of the nature of man and the purpose for human existence, will create the basic pattern of social life.

Literature is the nucleus of the story system. The stories that are fixed, preserved, and disseminated through the application of technology—for example, memorization technology, film, writing—are literature. Without literature no story tradition could grow by accretion; no story could be repeatedly transmitted to all or transmitted generation after generation with its identity intact.

The world in which people live, the world described by the story system, is a world created in literature. From the moment of birth one learns to live in this world through contact with the literature that created it. The family into which one is born is structured by and functions in accordance with the literary tradition of the group. The symbolic environment is based on literature. The content of the literary tradition is expressed in art and architecture, rituals, customs, manners, law, the schedule of work and leisure, in canons of ethics and morals, and in a thousand other ways. The members of a society absorb the literary tradition through a process of immersion.

Certain individuals and groups play a central role in the immersion process. They are people specially trained in the content and communication of literature. Their function is to maximize the impact of literature on the life of the group through direct presentations of the literature. The people who perform this function are communication specialists. All societies have them; they are the essential link between the literature and the people.

The role of communication specialists in society and the offices through which they perform their function are ultimately determined by the literature that has created the society. In primitive Greek and Norse societies, which were based on epic poems, the specialists were the memorizers and singers who preserved and recited the epics. In premodern Hebrew society, the specialists were scribes and rabbis. In medieval Christian society, the specialists were priests and preachers. In contemporary Soviet and Chinese society, the specialists are the party workers and the officials who see to it that the revolutionary tradition is presented to the people.

In American society the most important communication specialists are those who constitute the work force of three huge industries: the entertainment industry, the journalism industry, and the education industry. These three industries present the only literature that is disseminated to the entire society. The daily audience that each of these industries gathers numbers fifty to over one hundred million people.

The communication professionals who staff these industries are not the only communication specialists working in American society. There are others who present the literary traditions of various religious and ethnic groups to members of those groups. Before technology and compulsory education created the mass audiences of the entertainment, journalism, and education industries, the influence of the literature presented by communication specialists of the various religious and ethnic groups was powerful. Their audiences now, however, are incorporated into the mass audiences of the communication industries; their religious and ethnic traditions are engaged in an unequal competition with the literature disseminated by these industries. The confrontation between evolutionary doctrines and the Christian doctrine of special creation that was discussed earlier is illustrative of the competition in progress throughout American society. There is no enclave untouched by the stories of changing sexual morality (birth control, abortion, premarital sex), women's liberation, civil rights, and science, which have been disseminated throughout the society by the entertainment, journalism, and education industries.

These industries present the only literature that reaches the entire nation. American political literature, the literatures of the natural and social sciences, the literature of art and of entertainment, can achieve national audiences only through these industries. The only real world that all Americans can share is the one presented in the literature that these industries disseminate. They play a critical role in determining the effect the different American literary traditions have on American society.

THE ENTERTAINMENT INDUSTRY

The entertainment industry in the United States is a vast and diverse industry that distributes vicarious experience to the populace. Only parts of the industry provide vicarious experience through literature: the radio and television broadcasting industries, the motion picture industry, the popular song industry, and the publishing industry—insofar as it distributes the literature of entertainment. Other enterprises such as the professional sports industry are also parts of the entertainment industry, but since they do not provide vicarious experience through literature, they are not included in this discussion.

The American entertainment industry reaches everyone. The electronic devices through which it distributes much of its literature are found in virtually all households. The television set, like the family Bible in devout Christian communities, is a standard domestic fixture. The television set enables the literature of entertainment to play an impcrtant role in creating the picture of reality that the community holds in common.,

Like other major industries in American society, the entertainment industry functions in accordance with American religious and political literature. The story that makes the industry possible and inspires its activities is the basic American story presented in the Declaration of Independence and established by the Constitution. The entertainment industry in America is a private enterprise; its basic objective is private profit. Its freedom to present literature in pursuit of profit is protected by law. American religious and political literature thus shape the nature and purpose of the American entertainment industry in the same way that communist religious and political literature shape the nature and purpose of the Russian entertainment industry.

The nature and purpose of the American entertainment industry determine its relationship to its audience. The basic purpose for industry operations is profit. Profit depends upon the size of the audience that the industry attracts. The chief concern the industry manifests for its audiences, therefore, is that they assemble. Unlike some other communication enterprises, the entertainment industry is not significantly concerned with edification, instruction, or indoctrination. If the audiences gather, that is sufficient.

The need to gather the audience determines the nature of the literature the industry presents. The only literature that can consistently gather a mass audience is literature that provides vicarious experience that everyone finds enjoyable, engrossing, or exciting. The presentations of mass entertainment are, therefore, generally limited to presentations that offer vicarious experience of heroism, conflict, violence, danger, and sex. The appeal of such vicarious experience cuts across all lines of class, sex, age, and education— even across cultures. Stories involving violence, danger, heroism, sex, and conflict are found in the literature of cultures all around the world and across time. They are the staples of entertainment. It does not matter that the stories are only marginally different from one another. Audiences can indefinitely enjoy essentially the same fistfight, shoot-out, love scene, chase, and battle of wits. They are provided day after day, year after year, in films, television programs, novels, magazines, and popular songs. The audience responses are strong, consistent, and inexhaustible.

These responses sustain the enormous popularity of entertainments involving crime. Such entertainments have been among the most popular in America for some fifty years. When Alice Payne Hackett conducted her last survey of American bestsellers about ten years ago, Erle Stanley Gardner was still the bestselling of all American novelists—159 million copies of 125 titles—and Mickey Spillane held the volume record for individual titles. Seven of his novels each sold over four million copies![1] The same responses that these books evoked are exploited by today's multitude of film and television cops and robbers.

The inexhaustibility of the audience response to certain types of vicarious experience, the twentieth-century electronic technology, and the American principles of freedom that have left the entertainment industry unconstrained have enabled the American entertainment industry to do what no other entertainment industry has ever done: to make the literature of entertainment the most voluminously distributed literature among a population of over two hundred million people. No society has ever given itself over to the literature of entertainment as American society has. Books, magazines, and motion pictures are distributed nationally to vast audiences. The popular song industry fills the airwaves from coast to coast with its ballads. But the television industry has added the increment that makes the literature of entertainment the most widely distributed of all literatures in America. Over seventy million Americans watch television more than four hours per day.[2] Individual works of literature are presented to audiences numbering tens of millions at the same time, a feat never achieved before the advent of television. Television is a lifelong companion. It is in the nursery, it is present at the bedside of the aged and dying. No one is too poor, ignorant, unskilled, infirm, isolated, or lethargic to receive the literature of entertainment through television.

The effects of the literature of entertainment on any society are amplified in American society by the scale of distribution achieved by the American entertainment industry. Conventions and stereotypes of language, fashion, and beauty, of ethnic, regional, and occupational groups, of behavioral styles, and of every facet of national life that can be conventionally or stereotypically presented are disseminated nationwide. People who have never seen a Native American or a Puerto Rican know their stereotypes; people who have never heard ghetto dialects in their own surroundings can imitate them more or less fluently. The paragons of beauty are movie actresses.

The literature of entertainment often provides the only information people possess about some aspects of life. Many people's knowledge of fistfights, gun battles, and love affairs is derived mainly from entertainment. Many, especially young people, have no contact with any literature dealing with sex and intimate relationships that can compete with the literature of entertainment, particularly popular songs and romantic novels. The concepts many people have of the remote past, a reality accessible only in the literature, are created by the literature of entertainment. No historical literature ever produced had an audience impact in a mere twelve hours like that of the drama "Roots," which was seen simultaneously by an audience of over thirty million people.

In addition, many people have little contact, except through the entertainment industry, with literature presenting information about complex social realities. These people get their understanding of such things as police work, poverty, and the women's movement in much the same way that foreigners in the last century got their understanding of American slavery from *Uncle Tom's Cabin.*

Also, what many people know of the real world as described in the literature of knowledge is derived from entertainment. Many people's most significant encounters with psychology, law, medicine, astronomy, physics, and genetics occur in entertainments featuring psychopaths, lawyers, physicians, space travelers, and clones.

Finally, many of the emotional responses that Americans learn to express are learned from entertainment. We have already indicated the extent to which the development and expression of the emotions associated with romantic love depend upon entertainment. People also develop and learn to express emotional responses to many other realities of individual and social life. Emotional responses to violence, crime, ethnic groups, national enemies, and social problems are learned from entertainments. The only experiences some people have of such things are the vicarious experiences provided by the entertainment industry.

As the most thoroughly entertained society that has ever existed, American society is exposed to certain dangers. These dangers are inherent in the literature of entertainment.

Entertainment can degrade and desensitize the audience. No complex psychological theory is necessary to sustain this conclusion. If experience can coarsen and degrade, so can entertainment; for experience is what entertainment provides. The enormous growth of the market for increasingly violent and pornographic entertainment is sufficient evidence that entertainment can degrade people. Degraded behavior includes the appetite for such entertainment.

The appetite for higher levels of violence and obscenity increases as audiences become accustomed to lower levels. If the levels of violence and obscenity are not raised, the intensity of the experience diminishes; the audience is less willing to pay. Vincent Canby describes the action of the escalation process as it occurs in viewers of violent movies.

The more violent that films become in order to shock, the more violent they must become in order to continue to be shocking. The same graphic scenes of violence that penetrate dull brains, make those brains duller, more impervious to shock, so that succeeding films must go even further. The volume of screen violence must continue to be raised.[3]

The same escalation process operating in relation to pornography has recently produced a market for films presenting sexual acts involving young children. The evidence that entertainment can degrade could hardly be more conclusive.

The entertainment industry also exposes American society to the danger of illusion. Illusions are concepts that life experience cannot sustain or confirm. They become harmful when they lead people to undertake real life courses of action with negative individual and social consequences. The harmful illusions that the entertainment industry is most likely to propagate are those associated with its standard content: illusions concerning heroism, danger, violence, conflict, and sex. Heroism, sexual relationships, and violence are complex realities. When they are treated in entertainments, they are distorted and oversimplified. Anyone who knows these complex realities exclusively or predominantly from entertainment is certain to harbor potentially harmful illusions.

One illusion that the entertainment industry creates and disseminates is the efficacy of violence. In entertainment, violence solves problem after problem, allows justice to triumph, and brings conflicts to simple, emotionally satisfying conclusions. In Westerns, crime stories, and other violent genres the problems and conflicts are solved by killing or beating the people who are presented as the causes. It is gratifying to the vicarious participant to experience the destruction of the imaginary villain, whose acts have triggered responses of fear and hatred. Many Americans believe that certain grievous domestic and international problems could be efficiently and permanently solved by killing the people identified as their causes. Films like *Death Wish*, in which a wronged citizen becomes a street executioner, or the *Dirty Harry* series, featuring killer-hero Clint Eastwood, present the illusion of the efficacy of violence to large and receptive audiences.

The most prevalent and persistent illusion propagated by the entertainment industry concerns sexual relationships. This illusion is presented constantly in novels, love songs, films, and soap operas; virtually no one escapes its influence. The most harmful effect of this illusion is the belief that the turmoil of feelings and emotions that people experience when they "fall in love" can and should be permanent and that these feelings can and should sustain the marriage bond through life. The harm done by this illusion is evidenced in the instability of marriage and family life in the United States.

Societies generally take steps to minimize the dangers posed by their entertainment industries. Moral and legal constraints are employed to reduce the dangers of degradation and illusion. Certain forms of entertainment are outlawed, censored, or obviated by governmental control of the media. In the United States, legal restrictions are minimal. Although certain types of live entertainment like bullfights or other brutal spectacles are outlawed, presentation of the literature of entertainment is subject only to minimal restrictions.

Only two constraints serve at present to prevent the radio and television broadcasting industries from presenting the brutal and pornographic materials available in other media. These constraints, however, are self-serving and not inspired by any desire to protect the audience from degradation. One of these constraints is imposed by sponsors, who fear that audiences will hold them responsible for offensive content. The other is the fear of broadcasting corporations that the government licensing agency will accuse them of using the public airwaves irresponsibly if programming results in a public outcry. The application of both of these constraints depend on general public sensitivity. As this sensitivity is degraded by books, magazines, and motion pictures, the impact of these constraints becomes weaker; sponsors and broadcasters become more and more tolerant of degrading material, for their fears do not stem from any concern for their audiences' sensitivities but from fear of rejection of their products or of difficulties in renewing their licenses.

The laws prohibiting obscenity in books and films are ineffective The problem of defining the moral term *obscene* without a moral consensus has proved insuperable. There are no laws prohibiting the gross presentation of violence.

In America, constitutional guarantees of freedom of speech extend the protection of the law to offensive and dangerous literature of entertainment. The public, however, need not be without some means to protect itself from inadvertent contact with this literature. The practice of labeling is already established as a consumer protection device. The producers of foods, patent medicines, and cigarettes must indicate certain contents of their products. Some forms of entertainment are also labeled. Rating labels notify the public of explicit treatment of sex and sadistic violence in motion pictures. Certain books and magazines are labeled "adult," and their sale is restricted. Labeling of entertainments could be far more detailed and explicit and extended to entertainments produced for television. This would serve to protect children and to give adults a chance to make a conscious choice about the consumption of an entertainment.

Protecting society from the hazards of illusion is a less complex matter than protecting it from the hazards of degradation. The entertainment industry cannot be criticized for presenting illusions. That is its stock in trade. To insist that the industry present no illusions is to insist that all of its subject matter be presented without distortion, misrepresentation, or oversimplification, that it deal adequately with all the complexities of all of its subjects. It is to insist that the entertainment industry present the literature of art rather than the literature of entertainment. This is neither possible nor desirable. Entertainment has its own place in social life.

In order to prevent people from being victimized by the harmful illusions of entertainment, it is only necessary to ensure that entertainment is not the exclusive or predominant source of any information upon which any important action is based. Americans have alternative sources in abundance. The resources of knowledge and art of Western civilization are available. If the superficialities and distortions of entertainment play too great a role in social life, it is not because other resources are lacking but because they are not sufficiently utilized. The social and institutional structures whose function it is to distribute the literatures of knowledge and art are ineffective. A general failure to understand the importance of this literature makes Americans tolerant of its neglect. The field is left to the entertainment industry.

Even the most balanced observers of the entertainment industry in American society must acknowledge that Americans are over-entertained. They are too often and too intensively involved in vicarious excitement and pleasure. The illusions and the coarseness engendered by entertainment are too much in evidence. The material rewards, the high esteem, and the intense interest that performers receive betray a lack of perspective on achievement and a poverty of aspiration. The overgrown role that the literature of entertainment plays in American society is not, however, a consequence of the vigor and creativity of the entertainment industry. It is a consequence of the failure of the other sectors of society to make other forms of literature more influential.

THE JOURNALISM INDUSTRY

The basic function of the journalism industry is to distribute information about events that affect the public interest. This industry is among the largest in American society. It is comparable in size to the automobile and steel industries. It is larger than the drug industry. One sector of the journalism industry, the newspaper business, ranks tenth among all United States industries in the value of shipments. And the daily newspaper business is the nation's fifth largest employer.[4]

The journalism industry includes more than newspapers. The three major news magazines, *Time, Newsweek,* and *U. S. News and World Report,* have a combined weekly circulation in excess of ten million.[5] The wire services, Associated Press and United Press International, each serve more than four thousand clients in the

United States.[6] There are 719 television stations and over seven thousand radio stations,[7] all of which partly justify their use of public airwaves to the federal regulating agency by devoting at least 1 percent of broadcast time to news.

Like the entertainment industry, the journalism industry reaches everyone. Of all adults over eighteen years, 77 percent read a daily newspaper.[8] Forty-two million people watch the network news telecasts every evening.[9] Tens of millions also watch late evening local news telecasts. The journalism industry amasses the entire nation as its audience every day.

The American journalism industry is a product of the major American literary traditions, which create the special role and status of the industry. The literature that created and maintains the free enterprise system determines the organizational and financial structure of the industry. The literature of the natural and social sciences plays a major role in determining the content of industry presentations.

The journalism industry plays an important role in the American political system. The American political story confers sovereignty on the people and derives the power of the government from the "consent of the governed." One implication of this story is that the people have a right to know what is going on in the country, because they are sovereign. The people especially have the right to know what the government is doing, because the government rules by the consent of the people, and consent implies knowledge. The journalism industry is the link between the sovereign people of the political story and the government that serves them. The industry is not a branch of the government, although it is sometimes called the fourth branch. It is the part of the political institution that serves both the people and the government.

Another American literary tradition that has produced the journalism industry and determines its character and impact is the story of free enterprise. This story has made it possible, or imperative some would say, for the journalism industry to be a collection of private corporations operating for profit. American political stories make it impossible for the government to operate or control the journalism industry. And, just as government control has a critical impact on the type of literature a journalism operation produces, so also has private control. In the United States, such control creates the chain of consequences resulting from the relationship between the journalism industry and advertising.

The journalism industry is supported by advertising revenues. The quantity of revenues a news corporation is able to collect depends upon the size of the audience it attracts. Much of the literature that the industry produces, therefore, has no other purpose than to attract a mass audience and has no value apart from its ability to do so. Since the most reliable and efficient way to gather a mass audience is by providing vicarious experience, the journalism industry produces a large quantity of literature that is essentially entertainment. This literature is produced to attract a mass audience by providing vicarious experience of heroism, conflict, violence, danger, and sex.

The stories that provide this vicarious experience are so well established as standard news content that their presentation is taken for granted by both the industry and the audience. Few Americans, for example, wonder why the journalism industry presented the Longet case to the nation in 1976. Claudine Longet, a fairly well-known actress-singer, and the ex-wife of a famous performer, shot and killed her lover. The industry followed the story for months through the conclusion of her trial in a Colorado court. What is the purpose for all of this reporting? The events have no particular importance. The Longet homicide and trial are just another homicide and trial. Why does the industry inform the American people so fully about this one? Events with far greater public importance receive far less coverage, particularly by the electronic media.

The journalism industry treated the Longet story as it did because it is almost perfect entertainment. A beautiful, talented, well-known woman shoots the professional athlete with whom she lived after she had abandoned her famous husband. There are few Americans who would not respond with interest to such a story. It contains all the elements: the woman, her ex-husband, and her lover are all culture heroes (singers, performers, athletes); the woman is beautiful; her behavior is scandalous; her lover dies a violent death; she is arrested; the nation awaits the outcome of her trial.

The journalism industry does not acknowledge that stories like the Longet case and countless other less interesting stories of crime, sex, violence, and human interest trivia are produced to entertain the audience. Nor is it acknowledged that the media tell their audiences of murder, fire, storm, disaster, and flood because audiences take pleasure in the excitement such stories produce. Audiences are generally not aware that they respond to stories of crime, sex, disaster, and the like in the same way and for the same reason that they respond to fiction and melodrama. People would probably not wish to acknowledge that they derive satisfying excitement and pleasure from stories of crime or disaster. And yet one can hardly claim that his civic duty obliges one to keep up with such matters as the Longet case.

There can be no question of the importance of entertainment to the journalism industry. A survey taken by the American Newspaper Publishers Association shows that news items that entertain are the most attractive to audiences. The survey includes a listing of the categories "most widely read." Of the thirty-six categories identified in the survey, the most widely read of all is "accidents and disasters." Tied for third place are "crime" and "human interest."[10] "Advice columns" rank fourth. Among the eighteen to twenty-four age group the most widely read category is "comics."

If the journalism industry did not provide entertainment on a massive scale, the industry could not maintain its position in American society. The industry has huge resources, a great many expensive facilities, and many highly trained personnel. These enable the industry to gather information from all over the world and to distribute it thoroughly, quickly, and efficiently in a large country of over two hundred million people. The resources, facilities, and personnel are financed by advertising revenues. Without these revenues the industry could not exist in anything like its present form. The industry can collect these revenues because it can gather a mass audience by offering the excitement of vicarious participation in events happening all over the world.

The role of entertainment in the operations of the journalism industry is somewhat obscured because some of the entertaining stories that the industry produces are also stories of importance that affect the public interest. Consider two highly entertaining news stories: the Longet case mentioned earlier and the Israeli raid on Entebbe, Uganda, in 1976. The Longet case has no public significance; it is simply a captivating sex and homicide story. Though the events are of no public importance, people expect such stories to be published; the journalism industry has been publishing them for one hundred and fifty years, and almost no one asks why. If justification is called for, democratic values are offered. The event happened, it is said, and the people have a right to know what has happened. It is assumed that the public wants to know about such things, and this assumption is correct. The public wants to know because it is exciting to know about such things. The public enjoys the vicarious experience that such reports provide.

The situation relative to the Entebbe raid is a little more complicated. The story of the raid is as exciting an entertainment as the Longet case; it has all the elements of entertainment and can be enjoyed as such. Two fictitious versions of the raid were hurriedly produced for the prime-time entertainment audience; the entertainment potential was clearly perceived by the entertainment industry. But unlike the Longet case, the Entebbe raid also had political significance and involved the public interest. Sovereign states were involved; one of these, Israel, occupies a sensitive position in a part of the world where vital American interests are at stake. Almost everything Israel does outside its own borders is of grave concern to Americans.

Neither the public nor the journalism industry distinguishes the entertaining reports that are important, like that of the Entebbe raid, from those that are not, like that of the Longet case. All are covered by the obscure rubric *news*. The different functions and importance of the two types of entertaining reports are not perceived. Some entertaining reports are vital to the public interest; others gather the audience and are not important at all apart from that.

There is little doubt that the need to provide vicarious experience in order to gather a mass audience leads to the neglect of many important public matters. The television news operations are the worst offenders because their time is limited. When the most entertaining items have been presented, there is often little time left. Print journalism, however, has space for material in addition to entertainment, and if a print organ wishes to publish other material, it can.

Conventional political wisdom deplores the place of entertainment in journalism. Condemnations of the news media for sensationalism, triviality, and vulgarity are delivered daily. It is ironic that the same entertainment content that provokes these criticisms also enables the journalism industry to fulfill its political role. The importance, influence, and effectiveness of the journalism industry are all tied to the size of its audience. It is the size of that audience that makes the industry wealthy enough to support its operations in every corner of the nation and world. It is the size of that audience that gives the industry its political power. If the journalism industry stopped gathering its massive audiences by entertaining them, it could not gather them at all. The sensationalism, triviality, and vulgarity, which are so much deplored, sustain the industry's huge-scale operations, which in turn make it possible for the industry to assume its political and social role: gathering information from around the world for immediate dispatch to a sovereign people. If the industry did not exploit the human response to vicarious experience, operations on a scale approaching the present one would be impossible. The entertainment function is not, therefore, incompatible with the industry's social and political functions; it is essential to them.

Another major literary tradition that combines with the American political and free enterprise traditions to create the journalism industry is the scientific tradition. The scientific tradition provides the journalism industry with its conceptual background. That is, the industry accepts and uses the stories of the physical world and of human nature that have been created in the literature of the natural and social sciences. No editorials supporting animistic opposition to mining and agriculture appear in the press, and news stories associate crime with poverty and mental illness but not with original sin or temptation by the devil.

The scientific tradition also provides the journalism industry with a theory of knowledge. As applied by the journalism industry, this theory of knowledge is best described as naïve empiricism. It provides the epistemological basis for the journalism industry's characteristic literary product, the factual report. Naïve empiricism as applied by the journalism industry gives primary emphasis to "facts." People, it is supposed, are informed if they are provided with facts. Theoretical and historical background information is considered nonessential or, worse, tendentious.

Naïve empiricism also justifies the indiscriminate production of factual reports and obviates the need to develop canons of selectivity. After all, facts are facts. The job of the journalism industry is to give the people the facts, not to decide which facts the people need, not to theorize about which facts are important. The industry can thus present the sensational and the trivial along with vitally important information and argue with conviction that it is obliged to do so. This is a very important benefit provided by naïve empiricism. It enables the industry to provide the vicarious experience that gathers the mass audience without surrendering its dignity or laying itself open to the charge of pandering.

The American journalism industry thus derives its origin, mission, structures, and operational modes from the culture's literary wellsprings. American religious and political literature provide the industry with its social mission and organizational structure and determine the relationship of the industry to its audience. The scientific tradition provides the industry with a conceptual framework and with a theory of knowledge that provides the inspiration and justification for the industry's standard literary form, the factual report. The journalism industry is now one of the largest industries in the world's most highly industrialized society. The literature that the journalism industry presents is the only literature of knowledge distributed to the entire society every day.

The literature of journalism creates the only story of the nation and world at present that Americans hold in common. The collective consciousness that Americans have of events in the nation and world at present and of the state of the nation and world at present is produced by the journalism industry. The world that exists today beyond the limits of personal experience is the world described by the journalism industry. The events that occur on all the successive todays beyond the limits of personal experience are those described by the journalism industry. What kind of a real-world-today is the one described by the journalism industry? What characteristics are imparted to this world by the literature the journalism industry produces?

The industry's need to provide vicarious experience imparts the characteristics of melodrama to the picture of the real-world-today, which it disseminates to the American people. This world is a world understandable in simple terms. There are good guys and bad guys, right and wrong, winners and losers, good and evil. There is "the Free World," which somehow includes Brazil and South Korea. There are the "Captive Nations." When the United States fought in Vietnam, it was to protect the freedom-loving people of South Vietnam from the communist conspiracy to dominate the world.

As in melodrama, events in the real-world-today depend on persons, not on complex cultural or historical forces. News presentations abound with stories of people; a melodrama without characters is no melodrama at all. Stories with characters, on the other hand, provide objects for audience identification and easy access to vicarious experience. Much of the political power of the journalism industry stems from its role as a casting bureau for melodrama. The industry can make or break public careers by casting a player as hero, villain, or fool. Public figures realize this and try to appear as impeccable and true blue as dime-store novel heroes.

The journalism industry's transformation of public life into melodrama is most evident during campaigns and elections. The industry reconstructs them as stories of chase and contest. In order to keep the public interested for months, the industry uses such devices as polls, which keep a running score in front of the audience. Speeches, debates, public appearances, and the like are handled as opportunities to score points, make mistakes, win or lose. The audience loves spectacular misplays, fouls, master strokes. It is by reconstructing elections as melodramatic games and contests that the industry keeps its audience interested in the election reports.[11] If the industry published speeches and essays on the candidate's record and philosophy, they would simply be ignored. The public did not want a transcript of the Ford-Carter debates; it wanted a boxing arena-style decision naming the winner.

The story of the real world at present, which the journalism industry creates and which the American people hold in common, is a story strongly influenced by naïve empiricism. The journalism industry creates factual reports. It is naïvely assumed by the industry and its audience that facts are sufficient to provide understanding, that facts need not be set in a theoretical and historical framework. A report of a race riot in South Africa, for example, will give the location and time, the identity of the participants, the number of casualties, and, perhaps, mention of the incident that precipitated the riot. The riot is not understandable from such a report. There is no mention of the underlying cultural and historical factors. There is no moral or political theory to provide a basis for informed judgment. The riot has, for the journalism industry's audience, the aspect of a street fight at which the passers-by gaze curiously. Such reports are like the battlefield body-count reports that Americans watched on television for years during the Vietnam war. The war was always an enigma to the vast majority of Americans, even though it was the most closely covered war ever observed by the journalism industry.

Complex events cannot be understood from reports of facts. Men observed facts about the action of fire for thousands of years without coming any closer to understanding oxidation, and more observations and reports would not have helped. Social phenomena, like chemical reactions, only make sense in relation to theory. It is pointless to present large numbers of facts about such phenomena as crime, education, economics, and foreign relations without historical and theoretical material if the objective is to produce understanding.[12]

It is not possible for the journalism industry to provide more than factual reports of complex events. Factual reports gather the audience by providing vicarious experience and serve that audience by providing knowledge that an event has happened. Little more can be done. Historical and theoretical information is often boring, difficult, or voluminous. Television journalism as it is financed and organized in the United States is incapable of dealing with such information. Few, if any, newspapers other than *The New York Times* make any attempt. If the journalism industry were required to present historical and theoretical information, it would greatly increase the costs of production without increasing the size of the audience. The journalism industry could not provide the information necessary for understanding the events it describes without either pricing itself out of the market or forfeiting its mass audience.

The picture of the real-world-today that the journalism industry creates is thus a picture that is melodramatic, grossly oversimplified, or utterly mystifying. It is a real world, consequently, to which people respond emotionally, which they contemplate and discuss simplistically, or which they despair of ever understanding. The picture of the real world today created by the journalism industry hardly allows scope for any other kind of response.

The two communication industries we have considered thus far, the entertainment and journalism industries, exhibit important similarities. Both are very large industries; both have the entire nation for their audiences; both distribute literature that plays an important role in the life of the society; both attract their huge voluntary audience by offering vicarious experience. The two industries also distribute literature that produces gravely deficient pictures of the real world. There is only one communication industry in the United States that distributes literature that does not have the deficiencies of entertainment and journalism. That industry is the education industry.

THE EDUCATION INDUSTRY

The primary function of the education industry in the United States is to prepare the young for employment. This function is consistent with the character of American society. The United States is the most highly industrialized and technologically advanced society that has ever existed. The stability and continuity of social life depends upon large-scale efforts that prepare individuals for employment in the industrial and technical operations, which sustain the life of the society.

The education industry, like the other communication industries, reaches everyone.

> Education is in some ways the nation's largest business. In 1974/75 some 62.3 million of the total population of 211 million people in the United States were involved in education. This reaches almost 30 per cent of all the citizens of the country participating on a full time basis as either students or employees of the education enterprise.[13]

The primary function of the industry determines its relationship to its audience. The audience of the education industry is not made up of volunteers as are the audiences of the other communication industries. The first ten years of schooling are compulsory. This is in keeping with the importance of education in an industrial-technological society. The compulsion to continue education beyond ten years is less formal but hardly less effective. It is virtually impossible to obtain lucrative or prestigious employment with only ten years of formal education. Some of the audience attend only while compelled, but the majority remain because the education industry holds the key to employment.

In the process of preparing the young for employment, the industry performs another essential function. The industry propagates the religious and political creeds that are the foundation for certain basic patterns of cooperation. The transference of these creeds to the young is widely regarded as the primary function of the education industry. Commentators on the activity of the education industry refer to its function of "Americanization and unification." It is said that "nation-building has always been American education's mission," that a major goal of education is "the teaching of democratic ideals."[14] The most important aspects of the process of Americanization are inculcating the views of the nature and destiny of man and the purpose of society as set forth in the Declaration of Independence and inspiring confidence in and reverence for the constitutional-legal system that incorporates the religious story of the Declaration into social life. It is essential that these religious and political creeds be passed on to the young. Social cooperation depends on them.

Less often a matter of comment but equally important is the scientific creed. This includes the belief that the scientific stories of the cosmic order, material world, and certain social processes are correct, that reliable knowledge is acquired by the scientific method, that the authoritative source of information about nature and society is the literature of the natural and social sciences. We stated earlier that the patterns of cooperation that constitute such activities as mining, agriculture, and the exploitation of fuel and timber resources depend upon a view of the natural order and man's place in it. If people believe that the land must not be violated by ploughing and digging and that trees must not be killed, then agriculture, mining, and logging are impossible as are all forms of cooperation that depend on those industries. In the same way, a society officially accepts the guidance of economists in such vital matters as wages, prices, and interest rates only if the society believes that economists possess the most significant and reliable knowledge concerning such matters. A society permits psychologists to absolve individuals of responsibility for their actions only if the society believes that psychologists understand the nature of human acts better than any other authority. In Medieval Europe, the church taught that the authoritative source of information concerning nature, interest rates, wages, and human actions was theological literature. In American society, the education industry inculcates the scientific creed to establish the literature of the natural and social sciences as the authoritative sources.

In elementary and secondary schools, the education industry transmits the democratic and scientific creeds in the same way that societies have always transferred their basic creeds. They are presented as the only creeds worthy of belief, as the creeds that all informed and estimable Americans profess. The past is interpreted through the categories of these creeds; human political development culminates in American democracy; intellectual development culminates in science. A bright future is identified with progress in democratic forms and scientific knowledge. The literature on which these creeds are based is studied, but the goal of such study is to propagate the faith, not to make the young people expert in democratic and scientific literature. Relatively few Americans become expert in democratic and scientific literature, just as relatively few Christians became expert in Christian literature. As the history of Christian and other societies illustrates, it does not take much formal education to inculcate fideistic acceptance of views of reality that sustain basic patterns of cooperation.

The function of inculcating the democratic and scientific creeds is thus essential. It is secondary to the function of preparing the young for employment only in the sense that it plays a secondary role in organizing and directing the efforts of the education industry and in motivating the industry's audience. American schools and the process of education are organized in such a way as to move the young people through a series of well-defined stages to employment. The emphasis is on the importance of movement from one stage to the next and on acquiring the diplomas and degrees that mark the major stages. Progress is important for employment. If a young person did not quite finish high school, the fact that he had absorbed the democratic and scientific creeds would be regarded as of far less importance than the fact that his employment opportunities were drastically affected.

The primary and secondary functions of the education industry organize and regulate the presentation of literature by the industry. These functions determine which literature is selected for presentation, which literature is emphasized as most important, and which literature is neglected or excluded. These functions also determine the nature of the incentives that impel young people to study literature. By determining selection, emphasis, and motivation, these functions also create the attitudes of young people toward literature.

The literature at the disposal of the education industry for presentation is immensely rich and varied, the wealth of some three thousand years of creative effort. Only certain portions are selected for presentation. In elementary schools, the selection process is regulated, first of all, by the need to teach the children to read. Reading is an essential skill for employment in American society. In some societies, the reason for teaching reading is to render a particular body of literature accessible. Children were taught to read the vernacular or Hebrew so that they could read the Bible. Or they were taught Latin or Greek so that they could read the classics. The teaching of reading in American schools is not directed to providing access to any particular works of literature but to providing a skill necessary for employment. Proficiency objectives are not determined by the level of skill required to read a particular body of literature. Proficiency objectives are determined by employment objectives. Higher levels of skill are desirable primarily because they are necessary for higher education and the employment opportunities it provides. The literature that young children read in school is selected mainly because of its value for teaching reading. This is implied in the term *language arts*, which describes the courses in which literature is presented for the purpose of teaching reading.

Second in importance to the literature used to teach reading is the literature used to provide the mathematical skills necessary for employment or for further education in preparation for employment. The remainder of the literature that is emphasized in elementary school is simplified literature of the natural sciences that teaches the scientific creed, or it is the literature of history and "social studies" that teaches both the democratic and scientific creeds.

The literature that is neglected in or excluded from elementary schools is neglected or excluded because it does not assist the education industry in the performance of its major functions. Instruction designed to render the literature of foreign languages accessible is neglected; it is not necessary for employment or for teaching democracy or science. Classical literature is excluded because it serves neither of the industry's major functions. Some educators even regard classical literature as "elitist" and unsuitable for the education of youth in a democratic society. Theological literature is excluded or neglected because it is not necessary for employment, is in conflict with science, and is incompatible with democratic principles. The literature of music and art history are presented incidentally or not at all because they do not serve either of the industry's major functions.

In secondary schools, additional literature is presented because of the relationship of high school to employment objectives. High school divides the industry's audience into two categories: those who will go no further than high school and those who will go on to college. To those who will go no further, the high school presents literature that provides vocational training. To those who will go on to college, the high school presents literature necessary for admission. The study of foreign languages and of substantial scientific literature is directed toward college admission. Neither classics nor philosophy have vocational utility. Nor are they requirements for admission to college. They are, therefore, neglected.

The high schools continue to inculcate the democratic and scientific creeds. Ritualistic presentations of literature on the federal and state constitutions are common. So are required courses in American history. Many students also study textbook treatments of social sciences such as economics and psychology. Since many children terminate their educations with high school, it is essential that the democratic and scientific creeds be transferred by graduation.

By the time the young people reach institutions of higher learning, they are supposed to be adequately trained in the democratic and scientific creeds. The presentation of literature in colleges and universities, therefore, is directed almost exclusively to preparing the young people for employment.

Although colleges and universities present a range of literature much wider than is presented in elementary and secondary schools, selective criteria still operate. At this level, however, the criteria are applied by the individual who selects the school he wishes to attend and the program of study he wishes to pursue. Decisions are determined by employment objectives. Those who attend colleges and universities select the schools and study the literature which prepares them for a profession or vocation in medicine, law, engineering, commerce, or teaching. Many individuals who have not made specific employment plans study a variety of literature known collectively as "liberal arts." It is generally assumed that one who studies liberal arts does so primarily because of the uncertainty of his employment objectives. In such cases employment objectives are not served by the study of particular works but by the degree or credential that one earns through such study.

When relatively few people attended colleges and universities, the liberal arts degree alone was generally sufficient to ensure a wide range of employment options. In recent years, however, since the numbers attending colleges and universities have increased, the employment value of the degree alone has diminished; the emphasis is more sharply focused on vocational and professional training. This has led to a general decline in the numbers of people who concentrate on literature that provides no vocational training, such as classics and philosophy. In some colleges, classics departments have disappeared and philosophy departments are struggling to survive. One authority describes this situation:

> Concern for the humanities in higher education is growing. Over the years, university based humanists have watched ever increasing proportions of students, funds, and support going into the sciences and technologies. And now, pro-

grams leading students to immediate employment have arisen as the new competitors. Teachers of language, literature, and the arts cling precariously to the small part of the curriculum that is left to them. . . . Federal legislators . . . do not seem to care about the humanities. Nor do state legislators who welcome the opportunity to denounce "frill courses." And the students flock to occupational programs because they are told that they dare not graduate without training in a particular skill.[15]

As the emphasis on employment objectives grows, the study of the humanities declines because they do not serve such objectives.

The function of graduate education is exclusively to provide employment. It is extremely rare for an American to study literature at the graduate level if he does not intend to seek employment for which that study is an essential prerequisite. Many of those who achieve the doctorate culminate a twenty-year education process inspired every step of the way by employment objectives.

The desire for money, success, a "better life," and a higher standard of living has always organized and directed the lives of Americans. American materialism was originally inspired by the Protestant Ethic. American materialism was later secularized, and came to derive its inspiration not from theological sources but from the spirit of American democracy. The values of liberty and equality that give American society its special character have always included as essential aspects the freedom to pursue material goods and equality of opportunity in that pursuit. The pursuit of happiness involves as an essential aspect the pursuit of material goods. The literature that the education industry selects, emphasizes, and neglects reveals the profound influence of American materialism. The manner in which the industry motivates its clientele reveals the influence of this spirit even more clearly.

From the very beginning, children learn to view the education process as a lengthy preparation for work. In the early years, employment objectives are remote and are translated into concern with advancement to the next educational level. Children quickly learn that the purpose for first grade is to prepare one for second; the purpose for second grade is to prepare one for the third. Elementary school is preparation for high school, and high school prepares one for work or for college. The child understands that learning to read and learning arithmetic are important because they enable one to continue one's progress. The study of literature is essential because one must study it as required in order to pass. If one refuses, one fails. That is the only consequence of great importance.

The education industry also supplies more immediate incentives along the way. Grading and ranking systems import the spirit of competitive achievement into the education process. The value of study is identified with a place among the winners in an ongoing contest. In providing this incentive, the industry at once inculcates the values that are important for success in employment and motivates individuals to efforts greater than those needed merely to pass to the next level.

The problem with these incentives is that they are extrinsic. They condition the young to believe that intellectual effort and literature are valuable because they enable one to advance toward employment and to win in competition. These incentives effectively diminish or destroy the intrinsic value of literature for young Americans.

The major works of the literature of knowledge and of imagination that constitute the American literary heritage were not created to serve the purposes of employment or provide the basis for petty competition. This literature was created so that men might know truth and acquire experience, because truth and exprience are essential to right action and the quality of life. Philosophers, poets, novelists, theologians, moralists, and scientists all pursued these purposes. Their work was directed to the pursuit of truth as necessary for rational, ethical action, to spiritual objectives such as salvation or moral excellence, to the creation of acuity of perception and the fullness of experience that are essential for achieving personal and social grace and a higher level of existence, and to the pursuit of knowledge as an end in itself because understanding needs no practical objective to establish its value. Early scientists such as Copernicus, Galileo, and Kepler were inspired mainly by theological purposes. Galileo argued that nature, like the Bible, is a book composed by god, written in mathematical language, which is the key to understanding the divine revelation it contains. Kepler held that man can understand nature because he is created in god's image. The study of physics is "reflection on the divine ideas of creation; therefore physics is divine service."[16]

The American education industry uses literature to serve the industry's major functions. This service is not compatible with the nature and inspiration of much of the literature of knowledge that the industry presents; it is totally incompatible with the inspiration and purpose of the literature of art. The literature of art is not created to train workers nor to Americanize children. To use literature for purposes not in keeping with its nature and inspiration is to negate the intrinsic worth of this literature and to nullify the values created in it.

The objectives of the education industry are too narrow; it is not enough to prepare people for employment and to inculcate the democratic and scientific creeds. There are many beliefs in addition to the democratic and scientific faiths that must be shared if social life is to be harmonious, meaningful, and rich. There are many values in addition to success, liberty, and equality that are essential for social life, values such as truth, generosity, magnanimity, dignity, love, compassion, temperance, beauty, wisdom, civility, integrity, and many more. These values, like all others, are created in literature and should be transmitted through the process of education.

The process of education includes more than presenting works of literature, but presenting literature is essential to it. The proper presentation of literature involves appreciation, respect, and reverence for the intrinsic value of the content and utilization for purposes that are compatible with the content. Literature systematically used for purposes that are incompatible with its content is denigrated, subverted, and made to appear intrinsically worthless.

The employment function of the education industry is not its only problem. In propagating the democratic and scientific creeds, the industry also subverts and nullifies literature of great value and power. The scientific attitude that lays great stress on objectivity negates the authority of literature of imagination. Poetry and fiction, which analyze the human condition, are subjective and are not, therefore, adequate as sources of knowledge. Poetry and fiction may be enjoyable or even edifying, but the only trustworthy sources of knowledge of the human condition are the social sciences. Some teachers even assume the attitude that the whole matter of values is subjective and therefore outside the scope of serious intellectual effort. True knowledge, they say, is "value-free."

The objective spirit especially corrupts presentation of the literature of art. Analysis and criticism of works of art attempt scientific objectivity. Students spend their time analyzing plot structures, identifying themes, protagonists, or other objective features of works, and searching out historical influences. Questions of truth, value, and significance are not even raised. Students are forced to petty, irksome, and meaningless tasks by threat of examination. Works of literature are made the basis for performing in competition for grades. The intensive study of works of art becomes identified with boring and pointless nit-picking.

The presentation of works of the literature of knowledge and of art is further corrupted by the imposition of arbitrary and unrealistic time constraints. Young people are hurried from one work to the next so that they can "cover the material." Works that should be read and perhaps reread in an unhurried manner and savored and discussed along the way are read in great haste. Other works are read in rapid succession. It is impossible to enjoy or remember with pleasure the books read under such conditions. Books are read in this fashion for marks, credit, and credentials. Wisdom and enjoyment can hardly be the result of such a process. Reading under pressure for extrinsic purposes contributes substantially to the distaste for the reading of serious literature that young people acquire in school.

The quality of individual and social life in a society is determined primarily by the literary resources that create, sustain, and transmit the values that determine patterns of social life. If the quality of life in a society is degraded by violence, insensitivity to suffering, neglect of the young and the aged, addiction, alienation, and ugliness, it is ultimately because the society does not have or does not utilize the literary resources that can prevent or reduce these afflictions. Americans are generally aware of the importance and power of education. This awareness is expressed in the insistence that the education industry perform the functions assigned to it.

Americans are not, however, aware of the importance and power of literature and of the need to use literature to produce in the young a more comprehensive system of beliefs and values. It is not enough to prepare the young for employment and for cooperation based on a narrow range of beliefs and values. Success, liberty, equality, and scientific fideism do not encompass life, and if these beliefs and values are not permeated with others, they tend to assume degenerate forms. The pursuit of success tends to degenerate into the obsessive pursuit of money. The pursuit of liberty tends to degenerate into selfish insistence on one's own needs and wants and erodes the sense of duty. The pursuit of equality tends to degenerate into complacency and indifference to self improvement. Scientific fideism tends to erode the sense of mystery and wonder and leads to an exaggerated estimate of the competence of science. The values and beliefs that prevent such degeneracy are transferred to the young through literature properly presented. An adequate philosophy of education would adopt this as its first principle.

EPILOGUE: 4
THE LIBRARY
PROFESSION

The library profession bears a unique relationship to the human communication system. No treatment of this system offered to librarians and information scientists would be complete without a discussion of their profession. Our theoretical model of the human communication system provides the foundation for a theory of librarianship and the library profession. The purposes for which libraries and librarians exist become intelligible in the context of the general theory.

The library and the library profession originate with literacy. The library is to the literate society what the memorizer is to the preliterate society. The preservation of social and cultural forms, of knowledge and human experience, depend on the preservation of literature. The library performs the critical function of preservation, which is the keystone of civilization. In the present age, when literature is produced in unprecedented quantities, people take it for granted that nothing will be lost. And the library profession justifies this casual confidence in its capability.

In addition to preserving literature, the library profession undertakes the enormous task of organizing and controlling the vast literary resources committed to its care to make them accessible. The organizing and retrieval systems that the library profession has created enable the preserved literature to be used. Organization and control are essential if the sheer bulk of the material preserved is not to result in loss due to inaccessibility. Without the retrieval technology it has created, the library profession would be like the memorizer who knows every syllable of the sacred text but cannot speak.

Our theoretical model of the human communication system also makes it possible to understand the special character and functions of the library and library profession in American society and their relationships to the major social institutions, to literature, and to the communication industries.

The library and the library profession in the United States have a unique and essential political function. The democratic and libertarian principles that are fundamental to American social life require the existence of an information resource accessible to everyone without charge, controlled by no private interest, and constrained by no orthodoxy. The American religious commitment to freedom and to the autonomy of the individual demands that the political institution provide full and ready access to the intellectual resources that make freedom of choice and intellectual self-determination possible. The American library profession is dedicated to providing the nation with those resources.

The ordinary structure of distribution of these resources is the public library. No comparable agency exists. All others are either small in scale, selective in clientele, committed to private purposes, lacking in adequate resources, or dedicated to an orthodoxy. For the public library that takes its mission seriously, no significant work desired by a citizen is too ancient, inaccessible, exotic, dangerous, unpopular, impractical, unprofitable, radical, or repugnant. If a work is wanted, the public library is obliged to acquire it, preserve it, and offer it without question gladly. The library and the library profession are guarantors of the integrity of an essential element of the American religious and political creed. This indispensable service that the library profession aggressively and energetically performs is its most excellent contribution to American society.

The American library profession performs another service not as obvious as the others but of comparable importance. The library compensates for the deficiencies in the presentation of literature to American society as a whole, deficiencies that are results of the society's dependence on the three communication industries.

The library profession has an ancient and honorable commitment to the transcendent importance of literature. In the past this commitment inspired the profession's attitude toward preservation. Today the profession's commitment to the importance of literature is manifested in its concern for distribution. The emphasis is on doing everything possible to make literature accessible and to promote its use. The communication industries distribute literature primarily to make a profit and to prepare the young for employment. This limits the types of literature presented and forces literature to serve purposes incompatible with its content. However, the library offers the full range of literature and offers it for purposes that are consistent with its content.

The public library is the only agency that provides free nationwide distribution of the literature of art. Because of the library, access does not depend on one's financial resources or the proximity of a theater or bookstore. The entertainment industry presents the literature of art only when it is profitable to do so; the journalism industry does not present the literature of art at all; the education industry presents the literature of art to those who are in school but often presents it in a manner that negates and obscures its value. The public library, however, offers the literature of art to all in abundance without charge and offers it in a manner that does nothing to demean its value.

The library compensates for the deficiencies of the journalism industry by providing the resources necessary to understand the events that the industry reports. Anyone who takes seriously his responsibility for understanding public affairs can depend on no agency other than the library to make the necessary information available. Only the library is committed to offering, in sufficient quantity, information concerning complex events that represents the different points of view without favoring any. The public library is an essential public affairs information agency in a society that depends on private profit-making organizations for news.

Finally, libraries compensate for deficiencies in the education industry by providing resources for education in a manner consistent with their nature. Libraries do not subordinate the more important objectives of education to preparation for employment. Libraries offer no extrinsic incentives. They give no grades, exams, credits, or diplomas. The stance and attitude of librarians are the traditional ones that assert that literature is valuable because of its content. Within the education industry, members of the library profession attenuate the destructive aspects of the industry's attitude toward learning by bringing the attitudes and values of the profession into the schools and colleges. Often it is the librarian alone who is in a position to urge literature on the young people because they need it not for courses, credit, or employment but in order to live and grow. This is a most important service to education; it should be consciously and energetically provided.

It is essential that librarians and other communication professionals understand the nature of the human communication system and the critical role played by literature. American society does not need another professional group working unconsciously or in ignorance, oblivious or indifferent to the deep human and social needs they are obliged to serve. The model of the human communication system, which this book presents, offers to librarians as well as other professionals the theoretical resources necessary to formulate policies and set priorities that are appropriate to the social importance of their work.

NOTES

CHAPTER 1

1. Marshall D. Sahlins, "The Social Life of Monkeys, Apes, and Primitive Man," in J. N. Spuhler et al., *The Evolution of Man's Capacity for Culture* (Detroit: Wayne State University Press, 1959), p. 55.

2. Mead was born in 1863 and died in 1931. His life's work was done at the University of Chicago, where he arrived in 1893. Mead's contribution is *Mind, Self, and Society* (Chicago: University of Chicago Press, 1934). Vygotsky died in 1934 at the age of 38. His book is titled *Thought and Language* (Cambridge: MIT Press, 1962). Vygotsky's work was first published in Russia in 1934. Both of these books were published after the deaths of their authors. Mead's book was composed mainly from notes taken by students, one of whom had the foresight and initiative to employ stenographers, and from selections from unpublished manuscripts. It is a difficult book, to say the least, easily underrated or misunderstood. Vygotsky's book was suppressed in Russia in 1936 and did not reappear until 1956. These circumstances have contributed to the inaccessibility of the ideas of both men, an inaccessibility that has deprived their ideas of the appreciation they deserve.

3. Vygotsky, *Thought and Language,* p. 70.

4. The history of language clearly shows that complex thinking . . . is the very foundation of linguistic development. . . . If we trace the history of a word in any language, we shall see . . . that its meanings change just as in child thinking. . . . Transfers of meaning, indicative of complex thinking, are the rule rather than the exception in the development of a language. Russian has a term for day-and-night, the word *sutki.* Originally it meant a seam, the junction of two pieces of cloth, something woven together; then it was used for any junction, e.g. of two walls of a house, and hence a corner; it began to be used metaphorically for twilight, "where day and night meet"; then it came to mean the time from one twilight to the next, i.e., the 24-hour *sutki* of the present. Such diverse things as a seam, a corner, twilight, and 24 hours are drawn into one complex in the course of the development of a word in the same way as the child incorporates different things into a group on the basis of concrete imagery.—Vygotsky, *Thought and Language,* pp. 72-74.

5. Ibid., p. 5.

6. George Berkeley, "Concerning Human Knowledge," in Edwin A. Burtt,

editor, *The English Philosophers from Bacon to Mill* (New York: The Modern Library, 1939), p. 516.

7. Mead, *Mind, Self, and Society,* p. 141.

8. Ibid., p. 94.

9. Ibid., p. 95.

10. It is, of course, possible to learn some human activities by imitation the way young chimpanzees learn to fish for termites with a straw by watching adults. But wordless imitation is not the characteristic human way. No human child could ever learn the simplest arithmetic by imitation.

11. "The truth of the matter is that language is an essentially perfect means of expression and communication among every known people. . . . It is a fair guess that . . . its essential perfection is a prerequisite to the development of culture as a whole."—Edward Sapir, *Culture, Language, and Personality* (Berkeley: University of California Press, 1956), p. 1.

12. Colin M. Turnbull, *The Forest People* (Garden City, N.Y.: Anchor Books, 1962), p. 264.

13. Ibid., pp. 262-63.

14. Duncan Pryde, *Nunaga: Ten Years of Eskimo Life* (New York: Walker and Company, 1971), p. 34.

15. "Meaning is the content of an object which is dependent upon the relationship of an organism or group of organisms to it."—Mead, *Mind, Self, and Society,* p. 80.

16. Florence Rockwood Kluckhohn and Fred L. Strodtbeck, *Variations in Value Orientation* (Evanston, Ill.: Row, Peterson and Company, 1961), p. 4.

17. Mead, *Mind, Self, and Society,* p. 142.

18. Ibid., pp. 154-56.

19. Meaning is the content of an object which is dependent upon the relationship of an organism or group of organisms to it. . . . The social environment is endowed with meanings in terms of the process of social activity. . . . Certain characters of the external world are possessed by it only with reference to or in relation to an interacting social group . . . A social organism—that is, a social group of individual organisms—constitutes or creates its own special environment of objects.—Mead, *Mind, Self, and Society,* pp. 80, 89, 130.

20. Henri Frankfort et al., *Before Philosophy* . . . (Baltimore: Penguin Books, 1963), pp. 54, 75.

21. For a discussion along more traditional philosophical lines of the epistemological issues raised by our consideration of story systems, we recommend the essay by George A. Lundberg, "The Postulates of Science and Their Implications for Sociology," in Maurice Natanson, editor, *Philosophy of the Social Sciences: A Reader* (New York: Random House, 1963), pp. 33-72.

22. Emile Durkheim had a unique appreciation of the social importance of religion. "If religion has given birth to all that is essential in society, it is because the idea of society is the soul of religion."—Emile Durkheim, *The Elementary Forms of the Religious Life* (London: Allen and Unwin, 1915), p. 419.

23. Some scholars have defined religion in relation to information functions. Clifford Geertz, for example, defines religion as "a system of symbols which acts to

establish powerful, pervasive, and long lasting moods and motivations in man by formulating conceptions of a general order of existence and clothing these conceptions with such an aura of factuality that the moods and motivations seem uniquely realistic."—Clifford Geertz, "Religion as a Cultural System," in *The Religious Situation, 1968* (Boston: Beacon Press, 1968), p. 643.

24. Dorothy Nelkin, "The Science Textbook Controversies," *Scientific American* 234 (April 1976):33-39.

25. The progress of the story of evolution in Tennessee is noteworthy. In 1925 a teacher named John Scopes was brought to trial for teaching evolution. Fifty years later the creation concept that Scopes called into question was itself banished from the public schools.

26. Nelkin, "The Science Textbook Controversies," p. 39.

27. Thomas S. Kuhn, *The Copernican Revolution: Planetary Astronomy in the Development of Western Thought* (Cambridge: Harvard University Press, 1957), p. 191.

28. Ibid., p. 192.

29. John Donne, *Poetry*, selected and edited by A. L. Clements (New York: Norton, 1966), p. 73.

30. Kuhn, *The Copernican Revolution*, p. 199.

31. Ibid., p. 227.

32. Adolf Portmann, *Animals as Social Beings* (New York: Harper and Row, 1961), p. 231.

33. Sahlins, "The Social Life of Monkeys, Apes, and Primitive Man," p. 55.

34. John Locke, Jefferson's primary source for the philosophy of the Declaration, said, "The law of nature stands as an eternal rule to all men, legislators as well as others. The rules that they make for other men's actions must . . . be conformable to the law of nature, i.e., to the will of God, of which that is a declaration."—Locke, *Two Treatises of Civil Government* (New York: Dutton, 1924), pp. 185-86. John Dickinson was making the same point in 1766 when he said that rights and liberties are "not annexed to us by parchments and seals. They are created in us by the decrees of Providence, which establish the laws of nature. They are born with us; exist with us; and cannot be taken from us by any human power, without taking our lives."—In Gordon S. Wood, *The Creation of the American Republic 1776-1787* (Chapel Hill: The University of North Carolina Press, 1969), p. 293.

CHAPTER 2

1. Eric A. Havelock, *Preface to Plato* (Cambridge: Harvard University Press, 1963), pp. 42-43.

2. Philip K. Hitti, *The Arabs: A Short History* (Chicago: Regnery Company, 1970), p. 43.

3. The Canadian scholar Harold A. Innis argues that the process of development within a literate society is determined by the nature of the script and the materials used for writing. *See* Innis's *Empire and Communications* (London: Oxford

University Press, 1950), and *The Bias of Communication* (Toronto: University of Toronto Press, 1951).

4. *See* Havelock, *Preface to Plato*, p. 292, on the preservation of lyric poetry in ancient Greece.

5. Carlos Castaneda, *Journey to Ixtlan: The Lessons of Don Juan* (New York: Simon and Schuster, 1972), pp. 89-90.

6. "The history of American democracy is a gradual realization, too slow for some and too rapid for others, of the implications of the Declaration of Independence."—Ralph Barton Perry, *Puritanism and Democracy* (New York: Harper and Row, 1944), p. 133.

7. *See* Robert N. Bellah, "Civil Religion in America," *Daedalus* 96 (Winter 1967):1-21.

8. T. C. McLuhan, *Touch the Earth: A Self-Portrait of Indian Existence* (New York: Outerbridge and Dienstfrey, 1971), p. 15.

9. *The New Columbia Encyclopedia* contains a concise definition of scientific method that corresponds to the generally accepted notion.

> The scientific method has evolved over many centuries and has now come to be described in terms of a well-recognized and well-defined series of steps. First, information, or data, is gathered by careful observation of the phenomena being studied. On the basis of that information a preliminary generalization, or hypothesis, is formed, usually by inductive reasoning, and this in turn leads by deductive logic to a number of implications that may be tested by further observations and experiments. If the conclusions drawn from the original hypothesis successfully meet all these tests, the hypothesis becomes accepted as a scientific theory or law; if additional facts are in disagreement with the hypothesis, it may be modified or discarded in favor of a new hypothesis which is then subjected to further tests.—*The New Columbia Encyclopedia: Fourth Edition* (New York: Columbia University Press, 1975), p. 2450.

10. Quoted in Werner Heisenberg, "Tradition in Science," *Science and Public Affairs* 29 (December 1973):8.

11. Thomas S. Kuhn, *The Structure of Scientific Revolutions*, 2nd ed., enlarged (Chicago: The University of Chicago Press, 1974), pp. 174-210.

12. Heisenberg, "Tradition in Science," p. 8.

13. Kuhn, *The Structure of Scientific Revolutions*, p. 206.

14. Quoted in George A. Lundberg, "The Postulates of Science and Their Implications for Sociology," in Maurice Natanson, editor, *Philosophy of the Social Sciences: A Reader* (New York: Random House, 1963), p. 49.

15. Vernon L. Parrington, *Main Currents in American Thought,* Vol. I, The Colonial Mind (New York: Harcourt, Brace and World, 1954), p. 301.

16. Ibid., p. 352.

17. Henry Steele Commager, *The American Mind: An Interpretation of American Thought and Character Since the 1880's* (New Haven: Yale University Press, 1950), p. 211.

18. Ibid., p. 216.

19. Though always relatively obscure, Ward "raised up a school of disciples and his arguments came in time to be accepted as the common sense of the matter." —Samuel Eliot Morison, Henry Steele Commager, and William E. Leuchtenburg, *The Growth of the American Republic: Volume II*, 6th ed. (New York: Oxford University Press, 1969), p. 205.

20. Commager, *The American Mind*, pp. 214-15.

21. Some social scientists seem to acknowledge this. "If a psychology becomes socially established . . . it tends to realize itself forcefully in the phenomena it purports to interpret . . . psychologies produce a reality which in turn serves as a basis for their verification."—Peter L. Berger and Thomas Luckmann, *The Social Construction of Reality: A Treatise in the Sociology of Knowledge* (Garden City, N.Y.: Anchor Books, 1967), p. 178. See also E. Levenson, *The Fallacy of Understanding* (New York: Basic Books, 1972).

22. Havelock, *Preface to Plato*, p. 4.

23. Ibid., p. 207.

24. Ian Watt, *The Rise of the Novel: Studies in Defoe, Richardson, and Fielding* (Berkeley: University of California Press, 1967), p. 141.

25. "The conception of the feminine role represented in *Pamela* is an essential feature of our civilization over the past two hundred years."—*See* Watt, *The Rise of the Novel*, p. 162.

26. C. S. Lewis, *The Allegory of Love: A Study in Medieval Tradition* (New York: Oxford University Press, 1958), p. 4.

27. Watt, *The Rise of the Novel*, p. 135.

28. Denis de Rougement, *Love in the Western World* (New York: Harper and Row, 1956), pp. 287-296.

29. For a Freudian approach to the attractions of entertainment, see Simon O. Lesser, *Fiction and the Unconscious* (New York: Vintage Books, 1957), pp. 1-58.

30. Frank Luther Mott, *Golden Multitudes: The Story of Best Sellers in the United States* (New York: Macmillan, 1947), p. 121.

31. Ibid., pp. 118-21.

CHAPTER 3

1. Alice Payne Hackett, *70 Years of Best Sellers 1895-1965* (New York: R. R. Bowker, 1967).

2. George Gerbner and Larry Gross, "The Scary World of TV's Heavy Viewer," *Psychology Today* 9 (April 1976):42-45.

3. Vincent Canby, "Explicit Violence Overwhelms Every Other Value on the Screen," *The New York Times*, Section 2 (October 17, 1976):1.

4. Jon G. Udell, "Economic Trends in the Daily Newspaper Business 1946-1970," *University of Wisconsin Project Reports* 4 (December 1970):4.

5. *Literary Market Place* 1977/1978 ed. (New York: R. R. Bowker, 1977), pp. 554, 566.

6. John Hohenberg, *Free Press/Free People* (New York: Columbia University Press, 1971), p. 454.

7. U.S. Bureau of the Census, *Statistical Abstract of the United States: 1976,* 97th ed. (Washington: Dept. of Commerce, 1976), p. 536.

8. American Newspaper Publishers Association, "News and Editorial Content and Readership of the Daily Newspaper," *News Research Bulletin* no. 5 (April 26, 1973):19.

9. Jeff Greenfield, "The Showdown at ABC News," *The New York Times Magazine* (February 13, 1977):33.

10. "Letters to the Editor" rank second; "Obituaries" rank fifth. *See* American Newspaper Publishers Association, "News and Editorial Content and Readership of the Daily Newspaper," pp. 34-35.

11. Paul H. Weaver, "Captives of Melodrama," *The New York Times Magazine,* (August 29, 1976):6. "For television news is not primarily information but narrative; it does not so much record events as evoke a world. It is governed not by a political bias but by a melodramatic one."

12. While factual reports cannot produce understanding, they can produce awareness that an event has happened, and frequently this has sufficient value to justify the report. It is, after all, important to know that a manufacturer has poisoned the local water supply even if we cannot know why. So long as people do not mistake the knowledge that an event has occurred for an understanding of it, little danger exists.

13. Institute for Chief State School Officers, *Peak Use of Peak Years: A Report, Sponsored by the United States Office of Education* (Washington: U.S. Office of Education, 1976), p. 11.

14. *See* Fred M. Hechinger and Grace Hechinger, *Growing up in America* (New York: McGraw Hill, 1975), pp. 51, 416, and Wilbur B. Brookover and David Gottlieb, "Social Class and Education," in John H. Chilcott, Norman C. Greenberg, and Herbert B. Wilson, editors, *Readings in the Socio-Cultural Foundations of Education* (Belmont, Cal.: Wadsworth, 1968), p. 268.

15. Arthur M. Cohen, "Humanizing the Curriculum," *Change: The Magazine of Learning* 9 (June 1977):48.

16. Werner Heisenberg, "Tradition in Science," *Science and Public Affairs* 29 (December 1973): 4-10.

BIBLIOGRAPHY

Adler, Julius. "The Sensing of Chemicals by Bacteria," *Scientific American* 234 (April 1976):40-47.

Asimov, Isaac. *The Genetic Code*. New York: The New American Library, 1963.

Bellah, Robert N. "Civil Religion in America," *Daedalus* 96 (Winter 1967): 1-21.

Berger, Peter L., and Thomas Luckmann. *The Social Construction of Reality; A Treatise in the Sociology of Knowledge*. Garden City, N.Y.: Anchor Books, 1967.

Berkeley, George. "Concerning Human Knowledge" in Edwin A. Burtt, editor, *The English Philosophers from Bacon to Mill*. New York: The Modern Library, 1939, pp. 509-579.

Castaneda, Carlos. *Journey to Ixtlan: The Lessons of Don Juan*. New York: Simon and Schuster, 1972.

Cater, Douglass. *The Fourth Branch of Government*. Boston: Houghton, 1959.

Commager, Henry Steele. *The American Mind: An Interpretation of American Thought and Character Since the 1880's*. New Haven: Yale University Press, 1950.

Conant, James Bryant. *The Education of American Teachers*. New York: McGraw Hill, 1963.

Durkheim, Emile. *The Elementary Forms of Religous Life*. London: Allen and Unwin, 1915.

Fletcher, Ronald. *The Making of Sociology: A Study of Sociological Theory*, Volumes 1 and 2. New York: Charles Scribner's Sons, 1971.

Frankfort, Henri, et al. *Before Philosophy: The Intellectual Adventure of Ancient Man; an Essay on Speculative Thought in the Ancient Near East*. Baltimore: Penguin Books, 1963.

Geertz, Clifford. "Religion as a Cultural System," *The Religious Situation, 1968*. Boston: Beacon Press, 1968, pp. 639-688.

Gerbner, George, and Larry Gross. "The Scary World of TV's Heavy Viewer," *Psychology Today* 9 (April 1976):41-45, 89.

Hackett, Alice Payne. *70 Years of Best Sellers 1895-1965.* New York: R. R. Bowker, 1967.

Havelock, Eric A. *Preface to Plato.* Cambridge: Harvard University Press, 1963.

Hechinger, Fred M., and Grace Hechinger. *Growing Up in America.* New York: McGraw Hill, 1975.

Heisenberg, Werner. "Tradition in Science," *Science and Public Affairs* 29 (December 1973):4-10.

Hitti, Philip K. *The Arabs: A Short History.* Chicago: Regnery Company, 1970.

Hohenberg, John. *Free Press/Free People.* New York: Columbia University Press, 1971.

Innis, Harold A. *The Bias of Communication.* Toronto: University of Toronto Press, 1951.

_____. *Empire and Communication.* London: Oxford University Press, 1950.

Kluckhohn, Florence Rockwood, and Fred L. Strodtbeck. *Variations in Value Orientation.* Evanston, Ill.: Row, Peterson and Company, 1961.

Kuhn, Thomas S. *The Copernican Revolution: Planetary Astronomy in the Development of Western Thought.* Cambridge: Harvard University Press, 1957.

_____. *The Structure of Scientific Revolutions,* 2nd ed., enlarged. Chicago: The University of Chicago Press, 1974.

Lesser, Simon O. *Fiction and the Unconscious.* New York: Vintage Books, 1957.

Levenson, E. *The Fallacy of Understanding.* New York: Basic Books, 1972.

Lewis, C. S. *The Allegory of Love: A Study in Medieval Tradition.* New York: Oxford University Press, 1958.

Locke, John. *Two Treatises of Civil Government.* New York: Dutton, 1924.

Lundberg, George A. "The Postulates of Science and Their Implications for Sociology," in Maurice Natanson, editor, *Philosophy of the Social Sciences: A Reader.* New York: Random House, 1963, pp. 33-72.

McLuhan, T. C. *Touch the Earth: A Self-Portrait of Indian Existence.* New York: Outerbridge and Dienstfrey, 1971.

Mead, George Herbert. *Mind, Self, and Society.* Chicago: University of Chicago Press, 1934.

_____. *Selected Writings.* New York: Bobbs-Merrill, 1964.

Morison, Samuel Eliot, Henry Steele Commager, and William E. Leuchtenberg. *The Growth of the American Republic,* 2 vols., 6th ed. New York: Oxford University Press, 1969.

Mott, Frank Luther. *Golden Multitudes: The Story of Best Sellers in the United States.* New York: Macmillan, 1947.

Parrington, Vernon L. *Main Currents in American Thought,* 3 volumes. New York: Harcourt, Brace and World, 1954.

Pepper, Stephen C. *World Hypotheses: A Study in Evidence.* Berkeley: University of California Press, 1961.

Perry, Ralph Barton. *Puritanism and Democracy.* New York: Harper and Row, 1944.

Portmann, Adolf. *Animals as Social Beings.* New York: Harper and Row, 1961.

Pryde, Duncan. *Nunaga: Ten Years of Eskimo Life.* New York: Walker and Company, 1971.

Rougement, Denis de. *Love in the Western World.* New York: Harper and Row, 1956.

Sahlins, Marshall D. "The Social Life of Monkeys, Apes, and Primitive Man," in J. N. Spuhler et al., *The Evolution of Man's Capacity for Culture.* Detroit: Wayne State University Press, 1959, pp. 54-73.

Sapir, Edward. *Culture, Language, and Personality.* Berkeley: University of California Press, 1956.

Suzuki, D. T. *Zen Buddhism: Selected Writings.* Garden City, N.Y.: Doubleday, 1956.

Tawney, R. H. *Religion and the Rise of Capitalism: A Historical Study.* New York: Harcourt, Brace, 1926.

Turnbull, Colin M. *The Forest People.* Garden City, N.Y.: Anchor Books, 1962.

Vygotsky, Lev Semenovich. *Thought and Language.* Cambridge: MIT Press, 1962.

Watt, Ian. *The Rise of the Novel: Studies in Defoe, Richardson, and Fielding.* Berkeley: University of California Press, 1967.

Weber, Max. *The Protestant Ethic and the Spirit of Capitalism.* New York: Charles Scribner's Sons, 1930.

Wilson, Edward O. "Animal Communication," *Scientific American* 227 (September 1972):53-60.

Wood, Gordon S. *The Creation of the American Republic 1776-1787.* Chapel Hill: The University of North Carolina Press, 1969.

INDEX

ABOUT THE AUTHORS

Patrick Williams is Associate Professor in the Graduate School of Library Science at Rosary College, River Forest, Illinois. Joan Thornton Pearce is a principal of Mead Associates, Oak Park, Illinois. Together they have authored articles for *Library Journal, Catholic Library World,* and the *Journal of Communication.*